W9-AAJ-625

5 Ways to Know About You

Karen Gravelle

Illustrations by
Mary Lynn Blasutta

SCHOLASTIC INC.

New York Toronto London Auckland Sydney
Mexico City New Delhi Hong Kong Buenos Aires

No part of this publication may be reproduced in whole or in part, or stored in a
retrieval system, or transmitted in any form or by any means, electronic,
mechanical, photocopying, recording, or otherwise, without written permission
of the publisher. For information regarding permission, write to Walker
Publishing Company, Inc., 435 Hudson Street, New York, NY 10014.

ISBN 0-439-41779-1

Text copyright © 2001 by Karen Gravelle. Illustrations copyright © 2001
by Mary Lynn Blasutta. All rights reserved. Published by Scholastic Inc.,
557 Broadway, New York, NY 10012, by arrangement with Walker
Publishing Company, Inc. SCHOLASTIC and associated logos
are trademarks and/or registered trademarks of Scholastic Inc.

12 11 10 9 8 7 6 5 4   3 4 5 6 7/0

Printed in the U.S.A.   23

First Scholastic printing, May 2002

Book design by Chris Welch

We would like to thank Megan-Ann Gramlich, Willy Gramlich, Jessica Kiefer, and the Lincoln High School English/Humanities Magnet Class for sharing their writing samples for the "Handwriting Analysis" chapter with us.

Contents

Introduction

Have you ever wondered what makes you think, feel, and act the way you do? Or why you are so different from others in your family? Have you ever asked yourself how it is that you get along easily with some people but not with others? Is there a side of your personality that no one else seems to see? Does it sometimes seem like the most puzzling person you know is yourself?

If you've had any of these thoughts, you're not alone. Throughout history, people have struggled to understand themselves and others. Over time, folks from different cultures have developed systems for explaining what makes each of us unique and how we've come to have the personality and traits that we do. This book introduces you to five of these systems. The first four— astrology, palm reading, numerology, and Chinese horoscopes—began thousands of years ago. The fifth—handwriting analysis—is relatively new.

Each system uses a different technique and gives you a different slant on exactly who you are, so it can be fun to explore yourself by using all five. If you're like many people, however, you may find that you like one system best. If that's the case, you'll probably want to learn more about your favorite one. Fortunately, there is a lot more information available about all five of these ways of knowing yourself. In the back of the book, you will find some suggestions for places to look for additional information.

But first, let's start finding out who you are. Since some of you may already know your astrological sign, the chapter on astrology is a good place to begin.

Astrology

What the Stars Say About You

After countless years of gazing up at the stars, people in various parts of the world began to notice that certain heavenly bodies—the Sun, the Moon, Mercury, Venus, Mars, Jupiter, and Saturn—traveled regular paths across the sky. About five thousand years ago, early astrologers started to make predictions based on the positions of these bodies, or stars, as they were known. At first, these predictions were concerned only with large-scale events such as wars and floods. But around the time of the birth of Christ, the Greeks developed a way of predicting the destiny of an individual based on the position of the stars at the moment of that person's birth. Their method is the basis of the solar (meaning Sun) astrology system used today.

The idea behind this system is simple. The position of the stars when you were born is thought to influence your character and personality, as well as the timing of events in your life. (Although only the Sun is actually a star, astrologers still use this term to refer to the Moon and the planets too.) Since the stars are constantly moving across the sky, only a person born at exactly the same time and place as you were will have stars in the same position as you do.

At first glance, the idea that the stars can affect who you are may seem very improbable. However, as an example of how the stars might influence us, astrologers point out that the position of the Moon determines the tides of the ocean. More than 90 percent of the human body is composed of water. If the Moon can affect a huge body of water such as the ocean, then, astrologers argue, the Moon can certainly have an impact on our watery little bodies.

A complete astrological chart would show the position of the seven heavenly bodies known to the Greeks plus the more recently discovered Uranus, Neptune, and Pluto. The position of the Sun in your chart is by far the most important, however. By knowing what position of the sky, or constellation, the Sun was in at the time of your birth, astrologers can tell you what your basic nature is like, what your strengths and weaknesses are, and what kinds of people you are likely to get along with.

The second most important aspect of your astrological chart is your ascendant, the constellation on the horizon at the time of day when you were born. Your ascendant determines how you present yourself to the world. By combining your ascendant with your Sun sign, you can get a very good picture of exactly what makes you special.

Now that you know what astrology is about, let's see what your Sun sign and ascendant have to say about you.

Your Sun Sign

Finding Your Sun Sign

It's easy to find your Sun sign. All you need to know is the day and month you were born. The chart on page 35 will tell you what sign the Sun was in on your birthday. However, since a year is not exactly 365 days, occasionally a sign will begin a day earlier or later than listed here. Therefore, if your birthday is the first or last day of a sign and you don't think the description of your sign fits you, you might want to read the information for the adjoining sign to see if that is a better match.

Harmonious and Conflicting Signs

Before looking at the description of your particular Sun sign, it's useful to know which signs have things in common and which signs conflict. These similarities and differences have a lot to do with determining which people you're likely to get along with and which you may have more difficulty relating to. Learning these similarities and differences also helps you remember the traits of various signs.

One way that Sun signs are grouped is according to the element—fire, air, water, or earth—connected with them. People whose Sun signs are associated with the same element share a common nature. Since they are alike in important ways, they tend to get along well with each other.

The *fire* signs are Aries, Leo, and Sagittarius. Fire signs are energetic, enthusiastic, confident, direct, forceful, and often impulsive.

The *air* signs—Gemini, Libra, and Aquarius—are more concerned with thoughts and ideas. They rely strongly on their minds and on intellectual knowledge. They are also the signs most interested in communicating with others.

The signs associated with *water*—Cancer, Scorpio, and Pisces—are the most emotional signs. Despite the fact that they often have very good minds, water signs relate to the world primarily through their feelings and intuition. Their emotional nature gives these signs the ability to empathize with other people's problems.

Practical and stable are the words that best describe the *earth* signs, Taurus, Virgo, and Capricorn. These signs deal best with things and activities that have a concrete form, such as raising crops in a field, building a house, or administering money in a trust fund. The earth signs are literally the folks who bring plans and dreams "down to earth."

Astrological signs are also divided into three other groups according to another set of qualities that they share. Each of these three groups contains four signs that share common traits. However, in this case, people with signs in the same group are likely to have conflicts with each other rather than get along.

There is an exception to this general rule. Each sign in these four groups is directly opposite another sign. Two signs that are opposite each other in the zodiac are also opposite in personality traits. It's often the case that "opposites attract," primarily because opposite personalities each contain traits that the other lacks. Thus, two people with opposite Sun signs may complement each other's personality. Unfortunately, it's just as common for two opposite personalities to clash. Therefore, it's very difficult to predict how folks with opposite Sun signs will interact.

The first of these three groups are the *cardinal* signs—Aries, Cancer, Libra, and Capricorn. Cardinal signs are known for their ability to put their thoughts, feelings, and plans into action. For this reason, they are considered the "go-getters" of the zodiac.

The *fixed* signs are Taurus, Leo, Scorpio, and Aquarius. As their name implies, fixed signs are firm and not easily moved. These are the most consistent members of the zodiac, never deviating from the path they've chosen unless *they* decide to. Because they are able to concentrate their energy and maintain their focus, the fixed signs are very powerful.

The remaining signs—Gemini, Virgo, Sagittarius, and Pisces—are the *mutable* signs, the most adaptable of the zodiac. Their flexibility makes them easygoing, versatile, and able to adjust to changing circumstances.

On pages 6–30 you'll find descriptions of the twelve astrological signs. To help you get a complete picture of what the stars say about you, you may want to write down the key words describing your Sun sign in your personal star chart on page 40. You'll find this comes in handy later, when it's time to combine the information about your Sun sign with your ascendant.

Aries: The Ram
March 21 through April 20

As both a fire sign and a cardinal sign, Aries are *super* active. In fact, others may sometimes wonder if you ever sit still. In any event, they're likely to admire your enthusiasm, generosity, courage, and adventurous spirit. With your enterprising personality, quick wits, willingness to take risks, and eagerness to get started *now*, you are the pioneers of the zodiac.

Of course, even very positive traits like these can have a negative side. Your eagerness to get things going often makes you very impatient, and this impatience can make it much more difficult for you to accomplish things. Like a ram bashing its head against a wall, you may be in such a hurry to break down an obstacle that you overlook an opening where you could just walk through.

The famous Aries impatience can also result in a very quick temper. Fortunately, you are equally quick to forgive and forget, but others—particularly those born in water signs—may not be so willing to let bygones be bygones.

Ironically, although an Aries is the most likely to succeed in getting a project started, you can be among the least able to see it through. As a freedom-loving sign, most Aries hate restrictions and are bored to death by monotony. Unfortunately, once the initial excitement of a project has died down, it usually requires some fairly tedious work to complete it. This is when Aries individuals tend to lose interest and want to move on to something else.

If this sounds like you, there are several ways of dealing with this problem. One is to try to develop a little more patience so that you can actually finish what you start. Another is to choose projects that are short-term. That way, you have a chance of finishing them before boredom sets in. There is also a third solution that has worked for many Aries—teaming up with a partner who lacks the ability to get a project off the ground but has the staying power to finish the job. This enables the two of you to pool your strengths and make up for what each of you lacks.

Most people born in the sign of Aries crave physical exercise. With your strong competitive streak, many of you may be attracted to rough-and-tumble team sports such as basketball, football, and hockey. But just jogging a mile or two will do the trick as well.

There are any number of careers that Aries individuals can excel at, as long as the work is exciting in some way. Two of the most obvious are as a soldier or a firefighter. But if you don't feel like throwing your body in front of bullets or dashing into burning buildings, there are other ways of leading an exciting and challenging life. Perhaps you'd like to be an athlete, an explorer, an astronaut, a journalist covering stories in the far corners of the world, or a surgeon developing new ways of operating. The possibilities—like your energy, enterprising spirit, and enthusiasm—are limitless.

Aries individuals are most likely to get along with fellow fire signs, Leo and Sagittarius. You may also find good friends among those born in Gemini and Aquarius. In contrast, the other cardinal signs—Cancer, Libra, and Capricorn—may be more difficult for you to warm up to. The exception may be Libra, your opposite sign. People born in the signs of Aries and Libra may find that their personalities complete each other.

Taurus: The Bull

April 21 through May 21

Taurus and Aries are as different as night and day—which is to be expected, since Taurus is both an earth sign and a fixed sign. While Aries is full of fiery enthusiasm, bouncing from one project to the next, you are patient, persistent, steady, conservative, and slow to adapt to change. Chances are you are also strong-willed, stubborn, and determined. Add to these qualities your practical and reliable nature, and you can see why so many Taureans do well in business.

Not only are you skilled at making money, but you're good at holding on to it as well. This is fortunate, because possessions and material things mean a lot to those born in the sign of Taurus. In part, this is because these things help to provide you with a sense of security—and Taureans have a deep need to feel secure. But there's no denying that you like the good life. You have a love of luxury that includes beautiful things and good food.

In your relationships with others, you are warmhearted, affectionate, loyal, and trustworthy. But you can also be extremely possessive, treating your friends as if they were like the other things you own. Since possessions are so tied up with security for Taureans, people born in this sign can be very threatened by the potential loss of friends or material things. This fear is at the bottom of some of Taureans' less attractive traits—overpossessiveness, jealousy, and greed.

You are slow to anger, but like your symbol the bull, you can cause the earth to tremble when you finally explode. Once riled, you are just as slow to cool down. Often, it is something that has threatened your security that triggers the fireworks.

Taureans need to be careful not to carry persistence and single-mindedness too far. Otherwise, you may find you have become rigid and inflexible, with little ability to adjust to anything new. Perhaps the greatest pitfall for someone born in the sign of Taurus is the danger of falling into a rut without even knowing it.

As the earth sign connected with spring, most Taurus individuals prefer living in the country where it's possible to feel a connection with the land and growing things. In fact, many of you make your living as farmers. With your love of beauty and your joy in creating things with your hands, it's no surprise that many Taureans are successful architects, sculptors, builders, interior decorators, jewelers, artists, and art dealers. Working as a surveyor, a miner, or a real estate agent would also be a very practical way of being connected to the land.

In astrology, Taurus rules the throat. Thus, many people born in your sign have excellent voices and often become successful singers. But whatever the career, you're likely to be happy in a job that lets you take advantage of your practical and reliable nature, your desire to create something concrete, and your love of luxury and beauty.

People born in the sign of Taurus naturally gravitate to those born in the earth signs of Virgo and Capricorn. You will probably also get along with watery Cancer and Pisces. However, you're likely to have some fairly strong conflicts with the other fixed signs, Leo, Scorpio, and Aquarius. Keep in mind that while you may be very attracted to your opposite sign, Scorpio, both of you will have to be more flexible than usual if this combination is to work.

Gemini: The Twins
May 22 through June 21

The key word that describes Gemini is *changeable*. This changeability is both your strength and your weakness. On the one hand, it can result in a person who is extremely versatile, adaptable, and spontaneous. On the other hand, too much changeability is likely to make you inconsistent and superficial. The choice of how you use this trait is up to you.

Like all air signs, you relate to the world best through ideas—and you have plenty of those! The problem is that you often don't stick with any one thought long enough to develop it. Nevertheless, what Geminis sometimes lack in depth they make up in breadth. With your quick mind, you easily absorb information. Jumping from one interest to the next, you still manage to learn enough about a wide variety of topics to be a lively and interesting conversationalist—which is fortunate, because Geminis love to talk!

If you are like most Geminis, you have a strong urge to communicate. Used productively, this and your remarkable ability with words make you excellent journalists, teachers, writers, politicians, and salespeople. But you need to be careful that you don't talk just for the sake of talking, wasting too much time in gossip or idle chatter.

Like your symbol, the twins, you may often seem to be two separate people, moving in different directions at the same time. Geminis have a talent for juggling several things at once; thus, you may have two jobs simultaneously or a job and a full-time hobby. You may also have several careers over your lifetime, switching when your job becomes tedious or something more exciting catches your eye. If you're lucky, you may find a career that provides you with enough variety to hold your interest, such as being an actor or a news correspondent.

There's no denying that Geminis are popular with others. Charming, tactful, witty, amusing, and original, you're a lot of fun to be around. But your relationships with other people aren't deeply emotional. In fact, too much emotion makes you nervous. Thus, you're usually happiest in the company of the other air signs, Libra and Aquarius. You probably also enjoy Aries and Leo folks. On the other hand, your fellow mutable signs—Virgo, Sagittarius, and Pisces—are not as good a bet, although your best chances here are with your opposite sign, Sagittarius.

Cancer: The Crab
June 22 through July 22

As the first water sign of the zodiac, you are moody, sensitive, intuitive, imaginative, sympathetic, protective, nurturing, and sentimental. People

born in the sign of the crab see the world through their emotions—and your emotions can swing from one extreme to the other in a minute. This often makes it hard for others to know what to expect from you. With your wacky sense of humor, you can be the life of the party when you feel like it. But on a bad day, you're equally capable of making everyone miserable with your cranky complaining. Still, despite all your emotional fluctuations, you are intensely loyal to your friends and as likely to worry about their problems as your own.

In fact, worrying is something you do quite well. There can be a definite pessimistic streak in some Cancers and a tendency to expect the worst. In addition, many Cancers harbor a deep feeling of insecurity. No wonder you sometimes feel down!

However, beneath all your sensitivity and insecurity lies considerable strength. Like a crab that would rather lose a claw than let go of something, Cancers are incredibly tenacious. Once you start something, you are likely to finish it. And once someone or something has become important to you, you'll hold on to it for as long as possible. You also have an unusual kind of courage: You may not be very good at standing up for yourself, but you can be downright ferocious in defending others, particularly family members. This sometimes can take people by surprise.

Cancers are forever looking back to the past. No one is as attached to their childhood memories as those born in this sign. You've probably saved at least one favorite toy from your early days and you may still enjoy rereading a book you loved when you were little. Your love of the past probably gives you an interest in history as well.

Although Cancers occasionally can be wildly outgoing, you need time to be alone, time to spend thinking and living in your own very vivid imagination. You also have a deep need to keep a part of yourself private. With your sympathetic and caring nature, others may find themselves confiding their deepest secrets to you. But, while their secrets will be safe with you, it's not likely that you'll share all of yours with them.

Cancer is the sign of the home, and there's a good chance that you are quite attached to your home—it's both an extension of you and your family and a refuge from the world. Should your family decide to move, you will probably be the one who finds it hardest to leave your old house behind.

Which brings us to another contradictory aspect of your sign. Despite your attachment to your home and your past, Cancers have a strong streak of wanderlust. One way of satisfying your intense desire to experience different things is to travel. Thus, you're likely to do a lot of globe-hopping during your life, perhaps even living in various countries for a time. But if you're like most Cancers, in the end you'll probably return to the area where you were born.

Cancers are suited to a wide variety of careers. Your compassion, ability to empathize with others, and strong nurturing qualities would make you an excellent social worker, psychologist, teacher, or nurse. On the other hand, you may want to use your lively imagination and pleasure in creating fantasy worlds to become a writer or an actor. With your love of the past, many Cancers are drawn to careers as historians, antiques dealers, and archaeologists. Not surprisingly, Cancers enjoy being near the ocean. Thus, you may combine your love of travel and the sea to become a sailor, fisherman, or cruise ship employee.

You are most likely to be attracted to people born in Scorpio and Pisces, water signs that share your emotional nature. You're also likely to be compatible with those born in Taurus and Virgo. Folks born in your fellow cardinal signs—Aries, Libra, and Capricorn—may be harder for you to get along with, although many Cancers do quite well with their opposite sign, Capricorn.

Leo: The Lion
July 23 through August 23

Fiery Leo is impossible to overlook! Proud, regal, exuberant, dramatic, dazzling, and flamboyant, you love being the center of attention. Like the king of beasts, Leos need to rule—whether as captain of the football team, lead singer of a band, or homecoming queen. Fortunately, you are a natural leader whom others readily follow. You have more than your share of charisma, making it easy for you to win others to your side, and your generous, enthusiastic, and optimistic character inspires their loyalty. If that weren't enough, Leos are ambitious, hardworking, and exceptionally good organizers, so it's no wonder that you are so often found at the top.

In case all this sounds too good to be true, it's important to keep in mind that the negative side of Leo can be just as striking. Often, Leos want to rule *everything* and *everyone* in sight, and others soon resent being bullied and dominated. As a fixed sign, you also run the risk of becoming rigid and intolerant. And while the Leo self-confidence is an admirable thing, too much can turn you into a conceited, vain, arrogant, and snobbish person.

Still, most of the time, your warm, affectionate, loyal, and sunny nature makes you a great friend and a fun companion. Because of your supreme self-assurance, however, others may not realize how sensitive you are and how easily your feelings can be hurt. Not that you're likely to show it, unless someone has really injured your pride. Then your Leo rage will let everyone around know you've been offended.

From the description of Leo's traits, you can probably guess what careers you are likely to be attracted to. With your dramatic creative talents and desire to be in the limelight, you may enjoy being in show business as an actor, dancer, director, or producer. Leos can also be found in the fashion industry as successful models or clothing designers. Artists—particularly those who work in bold colors—may also be Leos. Since you are particularly at home heading an organization, you may find yourself a general in the army, the CEO of a large corporation, or the boss of your own small business. Leos also make excellent teachers. As long as the job is stimulating, lets you express your natural enthusiasm and creativity, and provides the praise and acknowledgment you seek, you're likely to be happy, productive, and successful.

Leos find it easiest to relate to their fellow fire signs, Aries and Sagittarius. You should also get along well with Geminis and Librans. Not surprisingly, you're likely to clash with the other equally stubborn fixed signs, Taurus, Scorpio, and Aquarius. Despite the fact that Aquarius is your opposite sign, this is one case where opposites may be too different to relate well with each other.

Virgo: The Virgin
August 24 through September 23

All of your traits, in one way or another, stem from the Virgo search for purity and perfection. And for a Virgo, purity and perfection can't exist where there are loose ends, clutter, and uncleanliness. Of all the signs in the zodiac, your sharp analytical mind and precise nature make you the best at dealing with details. But that doesn't mean that you necessarily *like* details. What you don't like is imperfection. And nothing can be perfect if the tiny details haven't been taken care of. In fact, unfinished projects, dirty bathrooms, and mistakes in a school report actually upset your nervous system.

One side effect of the Virgo attention to detail is that it can make you very critical. You often have no problem pointing out to others the flaws in their work, a rip in their clothes, or the fact that they used a word incorrectly. Not surprisingly, friends may soon tire of your faultfinding. Not that it would necessarily make them feel better, but they are probably unaware that you are even harder on yourself than you are on them. Perhaps it's the fact that you see your own failings all too clearly that gives rise to the sense of inferiority and inadequacy that plagues many Virgos. This is probably why you also don't like to be criticized yourself. In your mind, your faults are already glaringly obvious—you certainly don't want them broadcast far and wide for even more people to see.

Virgos are usually extremely health conscious. Therefore, you are likely to take very good care of your body and to be concerned about your diet. In fact, many Virgos become vegetarians. If you do get sick, it's often not germs that have made you ill but worry, anxiety, or overwork. Unfortunately, the well-known Virgo tendency to worry often results in digestive and intestinal upsets, skin problems, and ulcers.

As you would expect, Virgos excel at any job that requires careful attention to detail. Therefore, you are often found working as secretaries, statisticians, analytical scientists, accountants, and inspectors. You are also well suited for anything having to do with health and hygiene, including careers as a nurse, dietitian, and dental assistant. You may also want to use your critical abilities to become a literary or theater critic.

In your relationships with others, there's no question that you are dependable and sincere. But what often gets overlooked is how genuinely helpful you are. If a friend's party is supposed to start any minute and she's nowhere near being ready, you'll pitch in to get things under control. You don't do this to be thanked or even so she'll like you—you do it because she needs help.

In addition to your helpfulness, you have a sweetness and gentleness that attracts others to you. You also can be extremely witty. However, others will have to pay attention if they're going to catch the funny throwaway comments you make with a totally straight face. Although you're usually not comfortable in large crowds, you're likely to have a circle of devoted friends. And despite your tendency to criticize, you rarely make enemies.

With your practical and down-to-earth nature, you're most at home with those born in the signs of Taurus and Capricorn. You may also find that you appreciate and enjoy Cancers and Scorpios. But you probably won't relate as easily to other mutable folks born in Gemini, Sagittarius, and Pisces. It's possible, however, that you and your opposite sign, Pisces, will find that your very different personalities complement each other.

Libra: The Scales
September 24 through October 23

As you might expect, airy Libra is very concerned with ideas. But for those born under this sign, beauty and harmony are equally important. The combination makes you a gracious, charming, thoughtful, and sometimes exasperating individual.

The easiest way for others to understand you is to look at your symbol. Scales are used to find a balance between two things. In the process, however, they tip first one way and then the other. Like the scales, Librans can swing up and down a lot before coming to a decision. Your shifts are not like those of Geminis or Cancers, however. Geminis bounce from one thing to the next because something new has caught their interest, while Cancers are responding to their ever-changing emotions. You, on the other hand, have the ability and the need to examine an issue thoroughly from all sides. In the process of doing this, you change your position constantly.

Being able to analyze a problem from all perspectives is an admirable quality, but it is definitely a mixed blessing. Because you see the advantages and disadvantages of both options a little *too* clearly, you often have difficulty in making up your mind. In fact, indecision is one of Librans' major problems in life. Incidentally, Librans often have the reputation of being lazy. However, it's usually not your reluctance to work but your difficulty in deciding what to do that gives this impression. Once you determine what you want, you have no trouble going after it.

With your Libran love of peace and harmony and your aversion to quarrels, you're a natural diplomat. This, plus your friendly and outgoing personality, makes you delightful company. However, be careful not to let your desire for harmony prevent you from taking a stand when you should. Many Librans have a need to be liked by everyone. If you are too dependent on how others feel about you, you may find yourself overly influenced by their opinions or reluctant to say anything for fear of alienating them.

Almost all Librans have a love of beauty and a well-developed artistic sense. This means that you're likely to have a fine appreciation for art and music, and you may have real talent in these areas as well. Many of you use your artistic abilities to become successful interior decorators, artists, beauticians, owners of art galleries, or fashion designers. With your keen mind, concern with justice, and ability to see all sides of an issue, you may also make a skilled lawyer. But perhaps the most obvious career choice for someone with your inborn tact and desire for smooth relationships is to become a diplomat.

You're likely to find your closest friends among those born in your fellow air signs, Gemini and Aquarius. Leos and Sagittarians should also be compatible with you. Less likely are Aries, Cancer, and Capricorn, although here again, your opposite sign, Aries, may be an exception.

Scorpio: The Scorpion
October 24 through November 22

Scorpio is the most intense sign of the zodiac. It's also the most mysterious. The combination makes you a very magnetic, intriguing, dynamic, and powerful person. However, you are not likely to try to use these traits to attract attention. On the contrary, you can be the most secretive people under the Sun. Scorpios understand very well that knowledge is power. Therefore, while you are usually quite interested in what others are feeling, thinking, and planning, you're not likely to let them know what's on your mind. That might give them an advantage over you, which is the last thing you want.

As a fixed water sign, you concentrate your emotional energy in a way that your fellow water signs, Cancer and Pisces, do not. The result makes you both extremely passionate about everything you attempt and determined to do nothing halfway. These qualities are evident not only in the things you do, but in your relationships with other people. Scorpios are intensely loyal to friends and loved ones and willing to risk life and limb to help them. You can also be surprisingly gentle and protective of those who are weaker than you.

However, while you rarely forget people who treat you well, heaven help those who cross you, particularly if you feel betrayed. As a Scorpio, you have the ability to plot for years to get revenge on an enemy, even if you hurt yourself in the process. If you're wise, you'll realize that too much emphasis on getting even wastes your own life and your chance to do things that are more productive.

While we're on the negative aspects of Scorpio, the other trait that can sour your life is jealousy. You are fiercely possessive of what you believe to be yours, regardless of whether it's a best friend or a spot on the volleyball team, and you bitterly resent it being taken away by someone else. As a result, you may feel extremely envious of others who have something or someone you feel *should* belong to you.

Most Scorpios have uncommonly penetrating minds. Like everything else about your sign, your intellectual interests run deep. You would rather explore one topic thoroughly than have a superficial knowledge of several. In addition to your excellent analytical abilities, you are also highly intuitive and can approach a subject from this angle as well. These qualities, plus your desire to unravel secrets and your fascination with human nature, make you excellent psychiatrists, psychologists, and detectives. You can also excel in medical research, archaeology, or any other career that requires a razor-sharp mind and the ability to figure out a puzzle.

Typical Scorpios have little fear of anything. In fact, you may actually be attracted to professions that involve some danger, such as firefighter, police officer, or soldier. On the other hand, you may choose to use your personal magnetism, powerful personality, and ambition to become a movie star or the head of a large organization.

With your strongly emotional nature, you most easily gravitate to Cancer and Pisces, although you also relate well to Virgo and Capricorn. However, you're likely to encounter personality clashes with the other fixed signs, Taurus, Leo, and Aquarius. Of course, you and your opposite sign, Taurus, may find yourselves attracted to each other, but it can be hard for two such determined and stubborn signs to get along.

Sagittarius: The Centaur
November 23 through December 21

While Scorpios are all secrets and mystery, Sagittarians believe in letting it all hang out. With you, "What you see is what you get." And what others see is your sincerity, direct approach to life, openness, friendliness, and optimism—qualities that endear you to almost everyone.

It's fortunate that your goodwill toward others is so obvious, because your frankness can get you in trouble at times. The problem is that you frequently don't think before you speak. You don't mean your comments to be insulting or hurtful, they just fall out of your mouth that way.

Your blunt speech is only one way you show your scrupulous honesty. In fact, you're so honest that on the rare occasions when you try to lie, you do such a bad job that no one is fooled. One of the few things that can cause you to lose your temper is to be accused of dishonesty. Then, like all fire signs, you can let loose with a devastating blast.

Sagittarians have an unquenchable intellectual curiosity and excellent minds. You love the challenge of an intellectual problem and the fun of exploring various solutions. Since Sagittarius is the sign associated with higher learning, many of you become teachers, professors, lecturers, philosophers, librarians, writers, publishers, and booksellers. Like your opposite sign, Gemini, you are extremely versatile and often function best if you have more than one thing to do. Frequently, you may hold two jobs simultaneously.

Despite your intellectual interests, no one would call you a bookworm. You need a lot of physical activity and love the outdoors. Sagittarians are usually very involved in sports, particularly those with a dash of risk attached—such as skydiving or car racing. You also have a passionate attachment to animals. Many horse or dog breeders and trainers are Sagittarians. Those of you lucky enough to have the right physical build may combine your love of sports, risk-taking, and animals by becoming jockeys. Other Sagittarians make excellent veterinarians.

More than most people born in other signs, you are very independent and need a lot of personal freedom. You have little tolerance for jobs, relationships, or situations that make you feel tied down. Perhaps this is one reason why Sagittarians like to travel so much. Not only is it hard to pin you down when you are on the move, but visiting other places gives you a chance to explore new horizons.

Your need to feel free results in one of your few negative traits—a tendency to be irresponsible. Procrastination and excessive risk-taking are the other characteristics that can cause you trouble.

Philosophical and spiritual issues of life are of great importance to Sagittarians. Thus, at some point, you may become very interested in religion. However, you're likely to be less concerned with official creeds than figuring out for yourself what you believe.

With your versatility and talents, there are many careers you can choose from in addition to those mentioned above. Since you love the thrill of performing and being in the spotlight, show business is a natural place for you. Sagittarians are also considered among the best salespeople and promoters of the zodiac.

As you've probably guessed, you're most likely to get along with those born in Aries and Leo, the other fire signs. Sagittarians can also be very compatible with Aquarians and Librans. You'll probably have more difficulty relating to people born in Virgo, Pisces, and Gemini, although you and your opposite sign, Gemini, may make good partners if you work at it.

Capricorn: The Goat
December 22 through January 20

Compared to descriptions of more flamboyant signs, Capricorns may seem rather dull. But make no mistake, in your case, "Slow and steady wins the race." Ambitious and disciplined, you eventually achieve your goals—which, by the way, have little to do with winning popularity contests. What you're after is respect and authority. You don't have to be out in front, getting all the attention. As long as you're the one actually running the show, it's usually okay with you if it's from behind the scenes.

Like your fellow earth signs, Taurus and Virgo, you are reliable, patient, and persevering. You also are extremely practical and interested only in ideas and projects that have a concrete usefulness. Capricorns are basically conservative and rarely take unnecessary risks. There's no need to, since you've carefully planned each step ahead in great detail.

Because you are naturally reserved and somewhat shy, others may overlook you at first. Hardly a party animal, you're usually much more comfortable with a few close friends than in a large group. Then too, you're serious and responsible—one of those kids who do their homework without being prodded. If all this makes you feel like a complete nerd, take heart. Capricorns also have the best sense of humor in the zodiac. It's not the fall-down-the-steps, lampshade-on-your-head type of humor, but a dry, tongue-in-cheek variety that can be extremely funny.

There's another advantage to being a Capricorn—your life generally gets better with time. Capricorn children often seem a little too old and a little too serious for their age. But strangely, people born in this sign frequently get younger in spirit as they get older. In fact, you often have more fun in your mature years than others your age. Similarly, while Capricorn youngsters tend to be weaker and more prone to illness than other children, you get stronger the older you get. And in the end, you're likely to live longer than those born in other signs.

Fortunately, you'll probably have the finances to enjoy your old age. Capricorns are very concerned with security, and for you that means money. You have a real talent for making money, keeping money, and investing money, and it's highly unlikely that you'll ever be caught short. In fact, your honesty and ability to handle finances would make you an excellent banker. Even if you don't do this professionally, there's a good chance you'll be elected treasurer of any organization you belong to.

Given your reserved nature, a surprising number of Capricorns go into politics, while many others work as civil servants or administrators of some kind. The ranks of successful businesspeople are also full of Capricorns. Other career possibilities include engineer, builder, teacher, scientist, or surveyor. Essentially, you're likely to do well in any job that requires thoughtful planning, attention to detail, the ability to handle responsibility, and consistent effort.

The biggest pitfall Capricorns face is a tendency toward depression. You outdo even Cancers in your ability to worry. This is a shame, because with your talents, there's very little you can't achieve when you put your mind to it, including developing a more optimistic outlook.

Your closest relationships are probably with the other earth signs, Taurus and Virgo, or perhaps Scorpio and Pisces. For various reasons, you and the other cardinal signs—Aries, Cancer, and Libra—are likely to rub each other the wrong way. Of course, the occasional exception may be Cancer, your opposite sign.

Aquarius: The Water Bearer
January 21 through February 19
Anyone who has been your friend for long has probably learned to expect the unexpected from you. Although Aquarius is a fixed sign, your unpredictable and unconventional nature hardly seems to fit the description.

But beneath your kind, soft-spoken, courteous, and tranquil manner, you are just as firm and determined as those born in Taurus, Leo, and Scorpio. No one can get you to change your mind about an idea you've determined is correct. And no one can convince you to do anything you don't want to.

Aquarians are the humanitarians of the zodiac. Idealistic, unprejudiced, and a firm believer in the brotherhood of mankind, you are extremely concerned about injustice, poverty, and discrimination. Moreover, you're willing to work to eliminate these problems. Many of your ideas are quite revolutionary, although in the case of violent rebellion, you're usually not the one to actually lead the charge.

Like all air signs, you have an inquisitive mind. But the Aquarian curiosity outstrips everyone else's. You want to know about everything and everyone, from what makes a clock tick to why a friend believes in ghosts. Your mind works on several planes—analytical, intuitive, and sometimes even psychic—resulting in ideas that are original, inventive, unique, and frequently ahead of the times. Aquarius is the sign of genius, and a high proportion of famous people are Aquarians or have an Aquarian ascendant.

Although you are friendly and fascinated by people, there is likely to be a distinctly detached quality in the way you relate to others. You are generally more comfortable in friendships than in closer relationships, and happier with a group of friends than with one individual. Thus, while you make a kind and loyal friend, others often find it hard to really get close to you.

Aquarians are even more freedom-loving than Sagittarians. You can't stand to feel pinned down, and even having to agree to a specific time for an appointment may seem too restricting. Feeling trapped in any way is enough to make an Aquarian flee, so others must recognize your need for considerable personal freedom if the relationship is to last.

It's one thing to be naturally unconventional, but sometimes Aquarians try a little too hard to be shocking, perverse, or eccentric. That and a tendency to become too rigid in your thinking are the most problematic aspects of your sign.

Any career that makes use of your originality and inventiveness, while allowing you some independence, can be a good choice for you. Scientist and inventor are two obvious examples of this possibility. With your desire to help people, you may enjoy humanitarian work, perhaps with the United Nations. Aquarians also make excellent sociologists and psychologists. In fact, you often have a strange calming effect on those who are mentally disturbed. Many Aquarians are drawn to careers that have to do with the heavens, from designing the next spacecraft to being an astronomer. Although yours is the most forward-looking sign in the zodiac, you are often interested in the deep past, perhaps in exploring ancient history as an archaeologist.

Aquarians have the most in common with those born in the other air signs, Gemini and Libra. You may be equally compatible with freedom-loving Sagittarians and can also get along with those born in Aries. However, as you can imagine, relationships with your fellow fixed signs—Taurus, Leo, and Scorpio—are likely to be difficult. Even your opposite sign, Leo, is not likely to be a good fit.

Pisces: The Fish
February 20 through March 20

Pisces is the most difficult of the twelve astrological signs to get a handle on. This makes sense
when you realize that Pisces is the sign of illusion
and delusion and of things that lack a concrete form.
That doesn't make these things—or you, for that
matter—any less real. It just means that they, and
you, have to be understood in a different way.

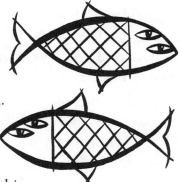

Of all the signs, Pisces is the most sensitive. And this
means sensitive to *everything*. One way your sensitivity shows is in your great
compassion for those less fortunate. Although those born in other signs may
also care about the poor or the troubled, you are unique in not judging people,
even when their difficulties may be their own fault. Somehow, you understand
human weaknesses and how easily anyone can slip and fall.

On the more negative side, you can also be the most susceptible to outside
influences, both good and bad. And bad influences can get you into very hot
water. Most Pisceans find reality a little difficult to take on an ongoing basis.
When real life becomes too ugly, too harsh, or too difficult, you have a strong
desire to escape. If you choose to escape into your own fantasies and dreams,
that's one thing. But sometimes Pisceans escape into alcohol or drugs. Of
course, you don't have to be born in the sign of Pisces to become addicted to
something. But drugs and alcohol can be a bigger temptation and more difficult
to shake for you than for others.

More productively, you may deal with the need to escape reality by using your glorious imagination and delicate sense of beauty to create art, literature, or music. Despite the fact that you shrink from competition, many of you are attracted to the stage, and a disproportionate number of dancers are Pisceans. Since theater, movies, art, poetry, fiction, and photography are reflections of reality rather than reality itself, they are natural fields for you.

You may also literally withdraw from life by joining a monastery or a convent. In fact, many mystics have been Pisceans. In addition to removing you from the real world, a religious life can fill a deep need many Pisceans have to make a sacrifice for others and to connect with a higher spiritual being.

Pisceans often have a vague, dreamy quality. In fact, if you're not careful, you may daydream your way through life. More than people of other signs, you have the tendency to delude yourself and to mistake your fantasies for reality. However, the dreams you have when you're asleep may be truly prophetic, alerting you to future events that will actually happen.

Your kind, compassionate, sensitive, artistic, romantic, and emotional nature is probably best appreciated by those born in the other water signs of Cancer and Scorpio. You may also find good friends among Taureans and Capricorns. But you are less likely to like Geminis, Virgos, and Sagittarians. The exception, of course, may be those people born in your opposite sign, Virgo.

Your Ascendant

Your ascendant is the constellation on the horizon at the time of day you were born. While your Sun sign describes your basic nature, your ascendant determines the way you express yourself to others. Thus, your ascendant is a good indication of how others see you. Your ascendant is especially influential in shaping people's first impression of you. As they get to know you better, your Sun sign traits become more obvious.

Your ascendant is also an additional clue about the type of people you feel most attracted to. *Regardless of your Sun sign, you are likely to get along with someone whose Sun sign is the same as your ascendant. Similarly, you will probably like someone whose ascendant is the same as your Sun sign.*

Finding Your Ascendant

To figure out your ascendant, you need to know the time of day you were born. In many states, the time of birth is written on your birth certificate, so that's a good place to start. If the time is not on your birth certificate, ask your parents or grandparents. At least one of them is likely to remember. To do a complete chart, astrologers need the exact time you were born, but for our purposes the closest hour will do.

Anyone can use the ascendant tables on pages 36–39. But since these tables are based on United States Eastern Standard Time, you'll have to do some additional calculations if you live in another time zone. If you were born in the Eastern Time Zone during the months when Standard Time is used (late October to late March), all you have to do is to look down the birth hour column until you find the hour closest to your birth time. Then look across that row until you spot your birth date. The heading above your birth date will tell you what your ascendant is. For example, suppose you were born at 10:15 A.M. Eastern Standard Time on November 25. Look across the 10:00 A.M. row (since that's the hour closest to your birth time) until you find the dates that include your birthday (in this case, Nov. 13–Dec. 12). Looking up, you can see that your ascendant is Capricorn.

It gets a little more complicated if you were born during the months when Daylight Saving Time is in force. Since the ascendant tables are based on Standard Time, you'll have to convert your birth time to Standard Time first. To do that, simply subtract an hour. Then use that time to find your ascendant.

Of course, you may not have been born in the Eastern Time Zone. If you were born somewhere else, first make sure that you've converted your birth time from Daylight to Standard Time, if necessary. Then determine the difference between your time zone and the Eastern Time Zone and add that to your birth time. (For U.S. Central Standard Time, add one hour; for Mountain Standard Time, add two hours; and for Pacific Standard Time, add three hours.) Use this new time to find your ascendant on the tables.

Regardless of where you were born, you can find your ascendant on these charts. All you need to know is the time difference between your place of birth and U.S. Eastern Standard Time. Be careful, however. If you were born in a country to the east of the U.S. Eastern Time Zone, such as Ireland, Poland, Venezuela, or Nigeria, you need to *subtract* the difference from your birth time to get your birth time in Eastern Standard Time. All the other steps are the same.

After you've read about your ascendant, enter the key words that describe it in your personal star chart on page 40.

Making Sense of Your Ascendant

Now that you've figured out what your ascendant is, what does it mean? Remember, your ascendant indicates how you express yourself to others. Therefore, if your ascendant is Leo, you present yourself in Leo-like ways—as an outgoing, self-confident, dramatic, creative, daring, and proud person. Of course, if your Sun is in a reserved sign, like Capricorn, there's a limit to just how dramatic and outgoing you can be—after all, you're still a Capricorn. In other words, your ascendant modifies your Sun sign, but it never replaces it.

Determining just how your ascendant blends with your Sun sign can seem confusing, particularly if the two astrological signs are very different. To learn how these two signs come together in you, examine the traits for your ascendant. Then look at your Sun sign traits again. Note the traits they have in common and list them in your star chart. For example, both a Scorpio Sun and a Pisces ascendant are very emotional. But signs that are very different in most ways may still have a few things in common. For example, fiery Aries and slow, steady Taurus both have hot tempers. After you've listed the traits that are similar, write down those that are different.

Any trait that your Sun and ascendant share will be doubly emphasized in you and should be very obvious to everyone. On the other hand, opposite traits can combine in various ways. In some instances, the two may meet in the middle. For example, a Capricorn with a Leo ascendant may seem warmer and more outgoing than most Capricorns, but more reserved than most Leos. On the other hand, the Leo ascendant may be more apparent at some times and the Capricorn Sun sign at others. If you're not sure, in your case, how conflicting traits blend, you may want to ask some people who know you what they think.

Your Astrological Profile

Now that you've determined how your Sun and ascendant work together to make you a unique individual, how well do you think your astrological profile describes you? Does it tell you anything about yourself that you didn't know before?

There are some additional things you can do with your astrological profile, if you want to. For example, it can be fun to compare your Sun sign and ascendant with those of your friends to see if your astrological profile accurately predicts the kinds of people you're most compatible with. Another interesting thing to do is to figure out your parents' and grandparents' Sun signs and ascendants. Frequently, astrological signs seem to be inherited. For example, you may find that your grandfather has a Virgo Sun, your mother (his daughter) has a Virgo ascendant, and you have a Virgo Sun. In this case, it would seem that Virgo "runs in the family."

Sun Signs

Aries	March 21 through April 20
Taurus	April 21 through May 21
Gemini	May 22 through June 21
Cancer	June 22 through July 22
Leo	July 23 through August 23
Virgo	August 24 through September 23
Libra	September 24 through October 23
Scorpio	October 24 through November 22
Sagittarius	November 23 through December 21
Capricorn	December 22 through January 20
Aquarius	January 21 through February 19
Pisces	February 20 through March 20

Ascendants

Birth Hour	Aries	Taurus	Gemini	Cancer
1:00 A.M.	June 6–June 26	June 27–July 17	July 18–Aug. 16	Aug. 17–Sept. 20
2:00 A.M.	May 23–June 10	June 11–July 2	July 3–July 31	Aug. 1–Sept. 5
3:00 A.M.	May 7–May 25	May 26–June 16	June 17–July 16	July 17–Aug. 19
4:00 A.M.	Apr. 21–May 10	May 11–June 1	June 2–July 1	July 2–Aug. 6
5:00 A.M.	Apr. 6–Apr. 25	Apr. 26–May 17	May 18–June 16	June 17–July 21
6:00 A.M.	Mar. 22–Apr. 10	Apr. 11–May 2	May 3–May 30	May 31–July 7
7:00 A.M.	Mar. 7–Mar. 25	Mar. 26–Apr. 15	Apr. 16–May 15	May 16–June 22
8:00 A.M.	Feb. 19–Mar. 10	Mar. 11–Mar. 30	Mar. 31–Apr. 30	May 1–June 6
9:00 A.M.	Feb. 4–Feb. 24	Feb. 25–Mar. 16	Mar. 17–Apr. 15	Apr. 16–May 23
10:00 A.M.	Jan. 20–Feb. 9	Feb. 10–Mar. 1	Mar. 2–Mar. 30	Mar. 31–May 7
11:00 A.M.	Jan. 6–Jan. 22	Jan. 23–Feb. 14	Feb. 15–Mar. 16	Mar. 17–Apr. 22
12:00 noon	Dec. 23–Jan. 9	Jan. 10–Jan. 30	Jan. 31–Mar. 1	Mar. 2–Apr. 6
1:00 P.M.	Dec. 5–Dec. 24	Dec. 25–Jan. 15	Jan. 16–Feb. 13	Feb. 14–Mar. 22
2:00 P.M.	Nov. 18–Dec. 9	Dec. 10–Dec. 30	Dec. 31–Jan. 29	Jan. 30–Mar. 5
3:00 P.M.	Nov. 4–Nov. 27	Nov. 28–Dec. 15	Dec. 16–Jan. 14	Jan. 15–Feb. 19
4:00 P.M.	Oct. 22–Nov. 8	Nov. 9–Nov. 30	Dec. 1–Dec. 28	Dec. 29–Feb. 4
5:00 P.M.	Oct. 6–Oct. 24	Oct. 25–Nov. 14	Nov. 15–Dec. 14	Dec. 15–Jan. 20

Birth Hour	Aries	Taurus	Gemini	Cancer
6:00 P.M.	Sept. 20–Oct. 9	Oct. 10–Oct. 30	Oct. 31–Nov. 29	Nov. 30–Jan. 5
7:00 P.M.	Sept. 5–Sept. 24	Sept. 25–Oct. 13	Oct. 14–Nov. 12	Nov. 13–Dec. 19
8:00 P.M.	Aug. 21–Sept. 9	Sept. 10–Sept. 30	Oct. 1–Oct. 30	Oct. 31–Dec. 6
9:00 P.M.	Aug. 6–Aug. 25	Aug. 26–Sept. 15	Sept. 16–Oct. 14	Oct. 15–Nov. 19
10:00 P.M.	July 21–Aug. 10	Aug. 11–Aug. 30	Aug. 31–Sept. 29	Sept. 30–Nov. 5
11:00 P.M.	July 6–July 21	July 22–Aug. 16	Aug. 17–Sept. 14	Sept. 15–Oct. 20
12:00 midnight	June 21–July 9	July 10–July 31	Aug. 1–Aug. 30	Aug. 31–Oct. 5

Birth Hour	Leo	Virgo	Libra	Scorpio
1:00 A.M.	Sept. 21–Oct. 30	Oct. 31–Dec. 7	Dec. 8–Jan. 15	Jan. 16–Feb. 23
2:00 A.M.	Sept. 6–Oct. 15	Oct. 16–Nov. 22	Nov. 23–Dec. 31	Jan. 1–Feb. 7
3:00 A.M.	Aug. 20–Sept. 29	Sept. 30–Nov. 6	Nov. 7–Dec. 16	Dec. 17–Jan. 22
4:00 A.M.	Aug. 7–Sept. 14	Sept. 15–Oct. 20	Oct. 21–Dec. 1	Dec. 2–Jan. 7
5:00 A.M.	July 22–Aug. 28	Aug. 29–Oct. 7	Oct. 8–Nov. 12	Nov. 13–Dec. 23
6:00 A.M.	July 8–Aug. 15	Aug. 16–Sept. 22	Sept. 23–Oct. 30	Oct. 31–Dec. 9
7:00 A.M.	June 23–July 31	Aug. 1–Sept. 6	Sept. 7–Oct. 14	Oct. 15–Nov. 22
8:00 A.M.	June 7–July 16	July 17–Aug. 23	Aug. 24–Sept. 29	Sept. 30–Nov. 8
9:00 A.M.	May 24- July 1	July 2–Aug. 8	Aug. 9–Sept. 15	Sept. 16–Oct. 24
10:00 A.M.	May 8–June 15	June 16–July 23	July 24–Aug. 16	Aug. 17–Oct. 9

Birth Hour	Leo	Virgo	Libra	Scorpio
11:00 A.M.	Apr. 23–May 29	May 30–July 9	July 10–Aug. 16	Aug. 17–Sept. 24
12:00 noon	Apr. 7–May 15	May 16–June 22	June 23–July 31	Aug. 1–Sept. 8
1:00 P.M.	Mar. 23–Apr. 29	Apr. 30–June 7	June 8–July 16	July 17–Aug. 23
2:00 P.M.	Mar. 6–Apr. 14	Apr. 15–May 24	May 25–July 1	July 2–Aug. 8
3:00 P.M.	Feb. 20–Mar. 29	Mar. 30–May 8	May 9–June 16	June 17–July 23
4:00 P.M.	Feb. 5–Mar. 15	Mar. 16–Apr. 23	Apr. 24–June 1	June 2–July 9
5:00 P.M.	Jan. 21–Feb. 26	Feb. 27–Apr. 7	Apr. 8–May 15	May 16–June 24
6:00 P.M.	Jan. 6–Feb. 13	Feb. 14–Mar. 23	Mar. 24–Apr. 30	May 1–June 9
7:00 P.M.	Dec. 20–Jan. 29	Jan. 30–Mar. 7	Mar. 8–Apr. 15	Apr. 16–May 24
8:00 P.M.	Dec. 7–Jan. 14	Jan. 15–Feb. 20	Feb. 21–Mar. 30	Mar. 31–May 8
9:00 P.M.	Nov. 20–Dec. 28	Dec. 29–Feb. 6	Feb. 7–Mar. 16	Mar. 17–Apr. 24
10:00 P.M.	Nov. 6–Dec. 14	Dec. 15–Jan. 21	Jan. 22–Feb. 14	Feb. 15–Apr. 7
11:00 P.M.	Oct. 21–Nov. 28	Nov. 29–Jan. 6	Jan. 7–Feb. 14	Feb. 15–Mar. 23
12:00 midnight	Oct. 6–Nov. 12	Nov. 13–Dec. 22	Dec. 23–Jan. 30	Jan. 31–Mar. 8

Birth Hour	Sagittarius	Capricorn	Aquarius	Pisces
1:00 A.M.	Feb. 24–Mar. 30	Mar. 31–Apr. 28	Apr. 29–May 21	May 22–June 5
2:00 A.M.	Feb. 8–Mar. 16	Mar. 17–Apr. 13	Apr. 14–May 5	May 6–May 22
3:00 A.M.	Jan. 23–Feb. 29	Mar. 1–Mar. 27	Mar. 28–Apr. 19	Apr. 20–May 6
4:00 A.M.	Jan. 8–Feb. 13	Feb. 14–Mar. 12	Mar. 13–Apr. 4	Apr. 5–Apr. 20

Birth Hour	Sagittarius	Capricorn	Aquarius	Pisces
5:00 A.M.	Dec. 24–Jan. 29	Jan. 30–Feb. 26	Feb. 27–Mar. 20	Mar. 21–Apr. 5
6:00 A.M.	Dec. 10–Jan. 14	Jan. 15–Feb. 10	Feb. 11–Mar. 5	Mar. 6–Mar. 21
7:00 A.M.	Nov. 23–Dec. 26	Dec. 27–Jan. 26	Jan. 27–Feb. 17	Feb. 18–Mar. 6
8:00 A.M.	Nov. 9–Dec. 14	Dec. 15–Jan. 12	Jan. 13–Feb. 2	Feb. 3–Feb. 18
9:00 A.M.	Oct. 25–Nov. 29	Nov. 30–Dec. 27	Dec. 28–Jan. 18	Jan. 19–Feb. 3
10:00 A.M.	Oct. 10–Nov. 12	Nov. 13–Dec. 12	Dec. 13–Jan. 4	Jan. 5–Jan. 19
11:00 A.M.	Sept. 25–Oct. 30	Oct. 31–Nov. 28	Nov. 29–Dec. 21	Dec. 22–Jan. 5
12:00 noon	Sept. 9–Oct. 14	Oct. 15–Nov. 10	Nov. 11–Dec. 3	Dec. 4–Dec. 22
1:00 P.M.	Aug. 24–Sept. 28	Sept. 29–Oct. 31	Nov. 1–Nov. 16	Nov. 17–Dec. 4
2:00 P.M.	Aug. 9–Sept. 10	Sept. 11–Oct. 12	Oct. 13–Nov. 2	Nov. 3–Nov. 17
3:00 P.M.	July 24–Aug. 29	Aug. 30–Sept. 27	Sept. 28–Oct. 20	Oct. 21–Nov. 3
4:00 P.M.	July 10–Aug. 14	Aug. 15–Sept. 11	Sept. 12–Oct. 4	Oct. 5–Oct. 21
5:00 P.M.	June 25–July 29	July 30–Aug. 27	Aug. 28–Sept. 18	Sept. 19–Oct. 5
6:00 P.M.	June 10–July 14	July 15–Aug. 11	Aug. 12–Sept. 3	Sept. 4–Sept. 19
7:00 P.M.	May 25–June 29	June 30–July 27	July 28–Aug. 19	Aug. 20–Sept. 4
8:00 P.M.	May 9–June 15	June 16–July 12	July 13–Aug. 4	Aug. 5–Aug. 20
9:00 P.M.	Apr. 25–May 29	May 30–June 27	June 28–July 19	July 20–Aug. 5
10:00 P.M.	Apr. 8–May 15	May 16–June 11	June 12–July 4	July 5–July 20
11:00 P.M.	Mar. 24–Apr. 29	Apr. 30–May 26	May 27–June 19	June 20–July 5
12:00 midnight	Mar. 9–Apr. 14	Apr. 15–May 12	May 13–June 2	June 3–June 20

The Stars and Me

Name: _____

Birth Date: _____

Birth Place: _____

Birth Time: _____

Sun Sign	**Ascendant**	**Comparing the Two**
(My basic nature)	(How I present myself; how others see me)	Traits in Common:
Traits:	Traits:	
		Traits That Differ:

2

Palm Reading

A Map of Your Life in the Palm of Your Hands

Palm reading is perhaps the oldest system of determining an individual's personality and character. Originating in India over five thousand years ago, it quickly spread to ancient China, Korea, and Japan. Much later, the practice made its way through Persia, Egypt, and Turkey, reaching Greece in the time of Alexander the Great.

Early palm readers concentrated on only the lines in the palm of the hand. Over time, however, other features of the hand became important as well. Today, an experienced palm reader will examine almost everything about your hands, from your wrist to your fingertips—including the shape of your hands, the length and shape of your fingers, the length of each of the three segments of your fingers, the line of your knuckles, the angle between your thumb and your palm, the shape of your fingernails, the size of the pads of flesh on your palm, the lines on your palm, and even your fingerprints.

Obviously, that's way too much for a book of this size. So, for a start, let's look at three of the most important indicators of who you are—the shape of your hand; the length of your fingers; and the head, heart, and life lines on your palm.

Which Hand?

The first step in palm reading is to figure out which hand to look at. The answer is simple. You need to examine both—not because they are the same (they aren't, by the way), but because each has something different to tell you.

Almost everyone has a major hand (the one you use to write a letter, hammer a nail, put on makeup, or throw a ball, for example) and a minor hand (the one you rely on less). Even if you consider yourself ambidextrous, or able to use both hands for most tasks, you probably have one hand that is a little stronger than the other. For most people, the right hand is the major hand and the left hand is the minor one. But if you are left-handed, your left hand should be considered your major hand and the right hand the minor one.

Your minor hand shows your potential abilities, or the possibilities you were born with. In contrast, your major hand indicates what use you've made of these abilities, or how your own choices and your environment have shaped these potentials. Since you are still relatively young, your hands probably don't differ that much. After all, you've barely begun to develop your potential.

The Shape of Your Hands

The shape of your hands says a lot about your basic personality. Generally speaking, hands fall into one of seven shapes—elementary, square, round, spatulate, philosophical, psychic, and mixed. Unfortunately, figuring out which shape best describes yours can be more difficult than it seems. That's because few people have hands that fit perfectly into one category or another. Therefore, what you're looking for is the description that comes closest.

Before you start, there are a few things you should keep in mind. First, in determining the overall shape of your hand, be sure to look at the palm side as well as the back, since the backs of most people's hands appear more square. Second, when determining the shape of your fingertips, look at the fleshy part, not the fingernail.

It's also a good idea to decide on the shape of your hands *before* reading the personality descriptions that go with the various shapes. If you are having trouble figuring out your hand shape, it can be tempting to choose the shape that seems to fit your personality. But that would defeat the purpose of reading your hands. After all, you're trying to find out what your hands say about you, not what you think your personality says about your hands.

If you are still confused after reading the following descriptions and looking at the illustrations, it can be helpful to compare your hands with those of your friends or your parents. Sometimes examining a variety of real hands can make it easier to determine what your own actually look like.

Elementary

The elementary hand is large, with a thick, heavy palm. The fingers are short and stubby and the fingernails are wide, rather than long. The thumb is thick as well. Sometimes, the elementary hand can look somewhat clumsy.

Square

The square hand is exactly that—square. The edges of the palm look straight, and the palm itself is square or slightly long. Although the fingers are usually short and square, they can also be long or thin. But whatever the fingers look like, the whole hand, including the fingers, should appear square. The palm has relatively few lines compared to the round hand, but the lines that are present are generally deep.

Round, or Conic

The round, or conic, hand is not actually round, but it has fewer straight edges than the square hand. For example, the outer edge of the

Elementary

Square

palm (the side opposite the thumb) is usually curved, and the fingers are long and tapering. Compared to the square or elementary hand, the round hand looks soft, light, and graceful. The palm usually has many lines.

Spatulate

The spatulate hand is a variation of the square hand, but it is more rectangular. One clear sign of a spatulate hand is a palm that is either wider at the base than at the top, or wider at the top than at the base. The fingertips are often flat or slightly bulging. The lines on the palm are deep and clearly cut.

Psychic

The psychic hand (see page 46, top) is an extreme version of the round hand, but it is longer and more slender. The fingers are slender and taper to a point. The palm is long and full of light, feathery lines.

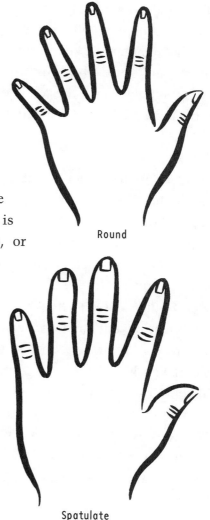

Round

Spatulate

Philosophic or Knotty

The philosophic hand (below) is easy to spot, with its pronounced knuckles, "knotty" finger joints, and generally bony appearance. The palm is often wider at the center than at the base or the top, and it is covered with many deep lines.

Mixed

Most people have hands that are mixed to some degree, but the mixed hand (see page 47) is *really* mixed. For example, the fingers may be completely different from each other, or the fingers and the palm may look like they belong to two different hands.

What Do These Shapes Mean?

The shape of your hands is the most important clue to your basic personality type. For example, if you have an *elementary* hand, you are likely to be an honest, hardworking person with a down-to-earth, commonsense approach to life. You are slow to change and can be very stubborn at times, particularly if others try to force you to do something you don't want to do. Most people

Psychic

Philosophic

with elementary hands enjoy working with their hands, and many are skilled at a craft or trade, such as car repair, furniture refinishing, or plumbing. But your strongest trait is your love of nature. You have an instinctive feel for animals and growing things, which would help you to be an excellent zoo attendant, pet trainer, farmer, or gardener.

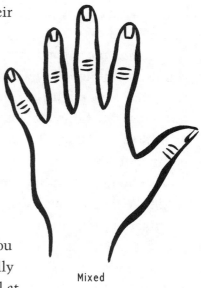

Mixed

A *square*-shaped hand indicates that you are practical, reliable, orderly, logical, methodical, patient, and levelheaded. Combine these traits with your determination and perseverance, and you can see why people with your hand shape usually achieve their goals. In fact, you're likely to do well at anything that requires organizational ability and attention to detail. Teaching, architecture, nursing, and business are just a few examples of careers that attract individuals with a square hand. Like those with an elementary hand, you tend to be on the conservative side and are often reluctant to try new things.

In contrast, those of you with *round* hands are creative, imaginative, and artistic. Many of you are talented painters, fashion designers, or interior decorators. Others of you may choose to use your imaginative powers in writing a novel or a screenplay. Chances are that you are sociable, warm, generous, sympathetic, impulsive, and a good listener. You're also likely to have a wide variety of interests, which is fortunate because you can become easily bored.

The *spatulate* hand is the sign of an unconventional, independent, self-confident, and inventive person with the potential to change the world, or at least shake it up a little. You're also probably very high-strung, restless, and full of energy. Although you can be a little eccentric at times, you tend to be well-liked by others. Interestingly, many people with a spatulate hand are natural musicians.

As you might expect, the *philosophic* hand belongs to the thinkers of the world. With this hand shape, you're likely to have great mental creativity, imagination, and originality, and you love using these abilities to analyze a problem or an issue. You're capable of a high level of concentration and can become completely absorbed in your work. In fact, the typical "absentminded professor" is a good example of someone with a philosophical hand. People with this hand shape are often college professors, researchers, anthropologists, and psychiatrists. Others use their analytical abilities to become theater critics or book reviewers. Although you often prefer to be alone, you're not antisocial. In fact, you can be quite entertaining and charming when you feel like it.

Not many people have a *psychic* hand, but those of you who do are extremely sensitive, idealistic, and trusting. The rough and tumble of today's world is a difficult environment for you, and you definitely don't do well in highly competitive situations. In fact, if there's anyone who has no business being a businessperson, it's you. On the other hand, you may have actual psychic abilities that can be used in helping others. You may also enjoy working in health and hygiene fields or in areas where a cultured taste is important, such as the fine jewelry or gourmet food industries. Many people who choose to enter religious communities have a psychic hand.

Since the *mixed* hand is a combination of different hand shapes, it's no surprise that people with this type of hand have a combination of traits. Thus, if you have a mixed hand, you're versatile, adaptable, and changeable. You thrive on challenges and are always willing to take a chance. With your flexibility, there is a wide range of careers that you may be good at. On the negative side, however, you can be inconsistent and often selfish.

Now that you have determined your hand shape and have a good idea what that says about you, you may want to write this information down in your personal chart on pages 67–68.

The Length of Your Fingers

Your fingers provide more clues about your personality. Their general length is determined by comparing your middle finger with your palm. Look at the palm of your hand. (When measuring, it's easier to see there where your fingers end and your palm begins.) If your middle finger is almost as long as your palm, your fingers are considered long. If it's less than three-quarters the length of your palm, your fingers are short. If your middle finger is somewhere in between these two measurements, your fingers are average length. In general, people with long fingers concentrate on details, while those with short fingers focus on the whole picture. Those with average-length fingers look at the two equally.

The most important information in your fingers is found by examining them separately. Each of the four fingers represents a different aspect of your personality. For example, your index, or first, finger tells a lot about your leadership abilities, ambition, and self-esteem. Your middle finger shows how responsible you are and whether your attitude toward life is serious or carefree. Your ring finger provides clues about your creativity and sense of well-being. Finally, your little finger reveals how you communicate with others.

To find out what your fingers say about you, you need to compare the

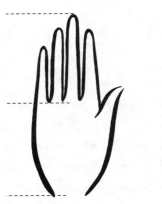

Long (middle finger almost as long as palm)

Average (middle finger slightly more than three-quarters the length of the palm but not as long as palm)

Short (middle finger less than three-quarters the length of the palm)

length of each with the length of the others. To do this, place your hands palm down on a flat surface with your fingers together.

Index Finger

Does the tip of your index finger (the finger itself, not the end of the fingernail) reach the bottom of the nail on your middle finger? If so, your index finger is of average length. However, many of you may have index fingers that are either longer or shorter than this.

Remember, your index finger indicates how ambitious you are, how much of a leader you are, and how you feel about yourself. If your index finger is of average length, you're not particularly dominating but you're not easily led either. If your index finger is longer than average, you're likely to be assertive, ambitious, very self-confident, and at least a little domineering. If your index finger is *very* long, you're flat-out bossy. A long index finger is commonly found in natural leaders and athletes. On the other hand, if your index finger is shorter than average, chances are that you are somewhat timid.

In the average hand, the index and ring fingers are about the same length. However, if your index finger is noticeably shorter than your ring finger, you can be rather cold and probably dislike having restrictions placed on you. You also hate to be criticized, although you have no problem being critical of others.

Middle Finger

Since the middle finger is the one used to judge the others by, it's a little harder to determine whether it's long, short, or average in length. A good rule of thumb (no pun intended) is to look at all the fingers together. In an average hand, the middle finger is the longest. In fact, it is often a nail longer than the ring finger. If the other fingers seem in proportion to each other and the middle finger is *especially* long, then you should consider it long.

In the case of a middle finger that is the same length as another finger, it's more difficult to determine whether it is short or the other one is long. Again, compare the middle finger to the hand as a whole. If the other fingers are in proportion (for example, if the index and ring finger are about the same length), then the middle finger is probably out of line and should be considered short.

The middle finger shows how you deal with responsibility. A long middle finger indicates that you are very responsible—perhaps a little too responsible sometimes. You may find yourself taking on other people's burdens or worrying too much about things that aren't under your control. A long middle finger can also be a sign that you are a rather lonely person. As you might guess, a short middle finger suggests that you have a more relaxed, fun-loving approach to life,

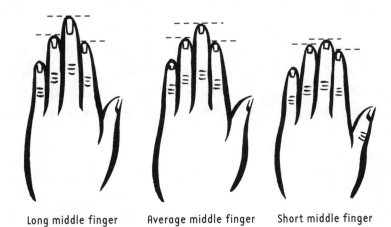

Long middle finger   Average middle finger   Short middle finger

but that you also have some trouble assuming responsibility. Those of you with a medium-length middle finger take a more balanced approach. You're willing to deal with your own responsibilities, but don't feel the need to shoulder anyone else's. And, while you're not the devil-may-care type, you're not overly serious either.

Ring Finger

The fourth, or ring, finger indicates creative talents. The ring finger is generally the same length as your index finger, but since it is often placed higher on your palm, it may pass the bottom of the middle fingernail. If your ring finger is longer than that, you probably have creative or artistic talent. Many of you with a long ring finger work as artists, art gallery owners, or art appraisers. You may also have considerable charisma, which can help to make you a good actor or entertainer. However, whether you will be financially successful using your creative talents is largely determined by your little

Average
ring finger

finger, since this finger indicates your relationship to money. In any event, consider your long ring finger a sign of luck, as people with a long ring finger tend to be optimistic, happy, and prosperous.

If your ring finger is of medium length, it doesn't mean that you aren't creative. It just indicates that you express your creativity more in your everyday life rather than focusing it on specific activities. You may also have creativity if your ring finger is shorter than average, but in this case, you're likely to have difficulty expressing it. Also, a short ring finger suggests that you are a bit pessimistic.

Little Finger

The average little finger reaches the joint between the middle and top sections of the ring finger. Little fingers that extend into the top section of the ring finger are considered long, while those that end somewhere in the middle section of the ring finger are short.

Average little finger

The little finger provides clues to how well you communicate. It also has a lot to say about you and money. The longer your little finger is, the more easily you express your thoughts in words. Thus, if you have a long little finger, you're probably very good at convincing others through what you say. If your little finger is very long, you may have a tendency to use your verbal ability to manipulate other people. In contrast, a short little finger suggests that you have trouble communicating your ideas and feelings.

Because the ability to communicate has a strong impact on a person's feelings of confidence, the length of your little finger may also show how much self-confidence you have. Thus, those of you with the ability to express yourself verbally are likely to feel confident as well, while those of you who struggle to say what you're thinking and feeling may often feel at a disadvantage.

There are other advantages to having a long little finger. If your little finger is long, you're probably good at making money, while having a short little finger indicates that you may have more of a financial struggle ahead of you. People whose little finger is of average length usually have enough money to be comfortable but aren't likely to become wealthy.

Thumb

The thumb is perhaps the most important feature that separates us from other animals. As you might guess, anything that significant probably has a lot to say about you. In fact, many palm readers feel that your thumb is the most important key to your character. Since your thumb provides much more information than can be included here, let's just look at clues provided by its length.

Average

The length of your thumb illustrates how much willpower you have and how you use it. To figure out the length of your thumb, place your hand palm down on a flat surface. Put your fingers together, then close your thumb against your palm. If your thumb reaches the middle of the bottom section of your index finger, it's of average length. If it extends beyond that, you have a long thumb. If your thumb

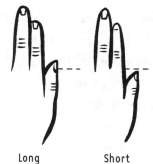

Long   Short

doesn't reach farther than the base of the bottom section of your index finger (or doesn't reach your index finger at all), it's short.

A long thumb is a sign of a natural leader. And like most leaders, if you have a long thumb, you're probably independent, stubborn, and in charge in most situations. You also have a lot of energy and are willing to go it alone if need be. A short thumb, on the other hand, is an indication that you are more of a follower. You're also likely to be someone who would rather accept the opportunities that are offered you than put your energy into going after something you really want. An average-length thumb suggests that you are a balance between these two extremes. You have the willpower to go after the things you want, but you have no desire to get others to follow you.

This is a good time to add the information your fingers and thumb have given you to your chart.

The Lines on Your Palm

For most people, palm reading is exactly that—*palm* reading. If you are one of these people, you have probably been looking forward to this section. You may also be a little nervous now that you're actually here. After all, if the lines on your palm say you are going to die young, you may not be too anxious to know this.

Well, take a deep breath and relax. Despite what you may have seen in the movies, none of the lines on your palm, including your life line, can tell you when or how you will die. For that matter, none of the lines, including your head line or your heart line, determine how smart you are or when or if you will get married. Instead, these lines describe the kind of physical, mental, and emotional energy you have or, in other words, how healthy you are, how your mind works, and how you respond emotionally to others.

To be able to see the lines on your hand clearly, you need a strong, direct source of light. You'd be surprised by how many lines you're likely to miss in regular room light, for example. If the lines on your palm are faint, you may even want to use a magnifying glass to get a better look.

In addition to making sure you have a good light source, there are several other things to keep in mind when examining the lines on your palm. While the length and direction of a line are very important, it also matters how clear or how pronounced the line is. For example, does the line cut a deep crevice in your palm or does it look more like a faint, feathery trace across the skin? Is it made up of one line only or is it a chain made up of several lines? Does the line fork or branch off anywhere? Each of these factors gives you additional information.

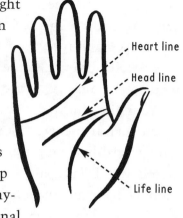

The lines on your palms are the things that are most likely to differ between your two hands. Remember, the hand you use least shows the potential abilities you were born with. The hand you use most indicates how you are dealing with these potentials.

Although most of the lines on your palm have something to say about who you are as an individual, the three most important are your life line, your head line, and your heart line.

Life Line

Your life line begins at the edge of your palm between your index finger and your thumb. From this spot, it swings around the ball of your thumb and continues down toward your wrist. In many people, the beginning of the life line is entwined with the beginning of another line that goes across the palm. (This second line is the head line, and we'll talk about it next.) In other folks, the life line is completely separate. Some life lines are quite short, while others may go all the way to the wrist.

Your life line indicates what your physical and psychological energy is like. That is, whether you are strong, healthy, energetic, and have a lot of physical stamina and endurance or whether you tend to be more delicate and have less energy and lower physical reserves to draw upon. If your life line is long and/or clearly etched on your palm, you're likely to have very good health and the ability to bounce back quickly from illness or injury. You're probably also blessed with an enthusiastic approach to life. On the other hand, if your life line is on the short side and/or is faint, feathery, or broken in places, you probably have less physical stamina and experience more trouble recovering from illness or emotional stress.

At this point, you may be thinking that your life line *should* indicate your life span, since there is certainly a connection between physical health and how long a person is likely to live. But remember, a strong constitution doesn't necessarily mean a long life. After all,

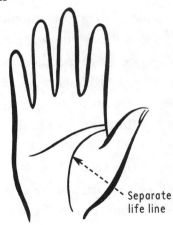

Entwined
life line

Separate
life line

the healthiest person can be killed in battle, during an earthquake, or as a result of an accident, while someone of frail health may be out of the country when a killer epidemic strikes.

Sometimes, a life line may appear to be short, but when you look more closely, there is a fine line that branches from it, connecting the life line to another line traveling toward the wrist. This usually signals a major change in the person's life, such as moving to another country or winning a lottery.

Where and how your life line begins is also important. If your life line starts high on your palm, closer to your index finger than to your thumb, you are likely to be a self-confident and ambitious person. Chances are, with this type of life line, you have leadership abilities. In contrast, a life line that begins close to the thumb suggests that you are more of a follower.

Whether or not the beginning of your life line is joined with your head line also says something about you. Look again at the illustrations on page 58. When the two lines are entwined at the beginning, it indicates that your parents have had a strong influence on you. If your life and head lines separate very shortly after they begin, you began to develop your own independence

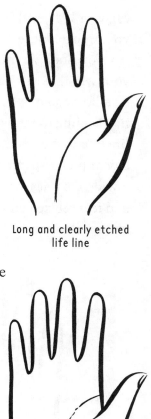

Long and clearly etched
life line

Short and feathery
life line

early in life. And if your life line is completely separate from your head line, you probably knew your own mind even as a baby.

Now look at the direction your life line travels as it moves down toward your wrist. Does your life line hug the ball of your thumb? If so, you're likely to be a homebody who enjoys the routine of a settled life. You have little interest in traveling to faraway places and even less in moving to a new town or state. A life line that hugs the ball of the thumb can also indicate that you are somewhat shy or prefer spending time alone. On the other hand, if your life line swings in a wide arc out toward the center of your palm, you like the company of others and feel relaxed and confident around them. If it swings *way* out, there's a good chance that you're someone who loves to travel to faraway places.

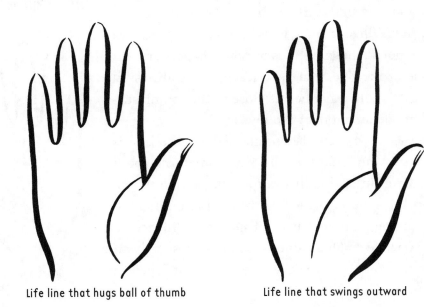

Life line that hugs ball of thumb   Life line that swings outward

Head Line

Your head line indicates how you think or, in other words, how your mind works. The head line begins at the edge of your palm between your thumb and your index finger, and travels across your palm. As mentioned above, in some people, the head line and life line are joined at the beginning. In other people, the head line and life line are completely separate, with the head line beginning above the life line. In a few people, the head line actually begins beneath the life line, then crosses the life line as it continues across the palm, as shown in the top illustration on this page. The head line can be short, ending somewhere in the middle of your palm, or it may extend all the way to the outer edge. It may move in a straight line or it may curve downward.

Head
line

Life
line

As you already know, if your head line and life line are completely separate, you are an independent person. However, a wide gap between the start of your head and life lines suggests that you're impulsive and often act without thinking. On the other hand, if your head line actually begins beneath your life line, you're probably an extremely cautious individual.

Short,
straight
head
line

A short head line is a sign that your mind is focused on very practical matters. If your head line is short, you're especially good at using your brain to make money or to solve concrete, everyday problems. Regardless of its length, a straight head line is another sign of a practical mind. In addition, a straight line suggests that you're able to really concentrate, since there's not much room for a short line to curve. Many people with short head lines also have head lines that are straight. This combination makes for a person who is practical, logical, and very focused intellectually.

A long head line, on the other hand, indicates that you have a more flexible mind and a greater variety of intellectual interests. Some people have long head lines that run straight across the palm. If this describes your's, you have the practicality and concentration that come from a straight head line, combined with the mental versatility of a long head line. But if your head line runs clear to the outer edge of your palm, it suggests that you are overly involved with details.

Instead of traveling straight across the palm, your head line may curve downward, toward the mound of flesh at the lower outside corner of your palm as shown in the illustration above. This area, called the mount of luna, is associated with imagination and intuition. The closer your head line comes to the mount of luna, the greater your imagination and creativity.

Many poets, writers, and artists have long head lines that swoop down toward the mount of luna. However, it's possible to have too much imagination. If your head line penetrates deep into the mount of luna, you need to guard against getting lost in fantasies and losing contact with reality. On the other hand, if your head line forms a gentle curve downward but doesn't reach the mount, you are able to use your imagination in a more practical way.

Of course, there's more to your head line than the length and direction it travels. It's also important to note how strong it is. A deep, cleanly cut head line is a sign that you are a clear thinker with no problems concentrating, while a chained, feathery, or wavy head line indicates that you are much more easily distracted and can quickly become bored. If you have a fine or faint head line but one that is also straight and cleanly cut, you probably focus clearly but can't sustain mental energy for too long at any one time.

Many people have head lines that branch at various points. A certain amount of branching is generally considered a good thing, for it gives a person mental versatility. If your head line branches into two relatively equal forks underneath your ring finger, it's an indication that you have strong talents as a writer. In fact, this kind of a branch is called a writer's fork.

Be careful not to confuse a branch in the head line with a line that starts somewhere else and then cuts through the head line. There are many lines that may cut across your life, head, or heart lines. Often, these lines start at the bottom of your palm, where they are sharpest, and travel upward. A branch, on the other hand, is a line that obviously forks off the line in question.

Heart Line

Although no one can predict when or how many times you will get married by looking at your heart line, this line does have a lot to say about your emotional nature and how you express your feelings for other people.

Your heart line begins at the outside edge of your palm, below your little finger and above your head line. From there, it runs toward your index finger, ending somewhere in the area of your index or middle finger. In a few people, the heart line and the head line are fused together and form one line that runs straight across the palm. Since their emotional and mental energies are combined, folks with a fused head and heart line tend to be very intense.

Straight heart line

If you have a straight heart line, you're probably somewhat cautious in romantic relationships and are likely to be more reserved in expressing how you feel. You may also have to shoulder responsibilities in love. A heart line that curves downward, on the other hand, is often a sign of someone who is fairly cold emotionally. In contrast, a heart line that curves upward indicates that you are a passionate, demonstrative person.

Where your heart line ends is also important. A straight heart line that goes all the way across the palm to the other edge suggests that you are in danger of putting work before your relationships, neglecting your family or others who are important to you. In comparison, a heart line that ends underneath your index finger shows that you are a born romantic. If it actually touches the bottom of your index finger, you probably have very high standards and expectations of love and of anyone you let into your heart.

Upward-curving heart line

In many people, the heart line ends in the webbed skin between the index and middle fingers. If this describes your heart line, you have an affectionate nature. However, while your emotions run deep, you'd rather express your feelings in actions than in words.

If your heart line ends under your middle finger, you're likely to have difficulty expressing feelings of love, period. This doesn't necessarily mean that you are a cold, unfeeling person. In many cases, people whose heart lines end below their middle finger are merely super cautious or afraid of getting hurt. Once they are sure their love is returned, they can make very loving and loyal partners.

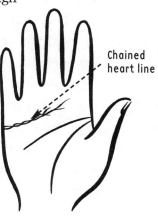

Branched heart line

Is your heart line a deep crevice in your hand or is it a light trace? A deep, strong heart line indicates that your feelings are also deep, regardless of how easily you express them, and that you are loyal in love. A lighter line suggests that your emotions are lighter or perhaps not very long-lasting. Chained heart lines are very common, probably because most people express their emotions differently with different people, but a heart line that is heavily chained can be a sign that your emotions fluctuate a lot or lack focus.

Lines branching from the heart line are also very common. Generally, lines that branch upward are a sign of happiness and success in relationships, while those that branch downward indicate some disappointments in love. This is one instance in which major differences may be seen between the heart lines on your two hands. When there are fewer downward lines on the heart line of the major hand, it shows that the person has learned how to avoid some of the mistakes that made earlier relationships fail.

Chained heart line

Now add the information you've learned from your life, head, and heart lines to your chart on pages 67 and 68.

Dealing with Conflicting Information

If you are like most people, there are probably some contradictions in the information your hands have given you. That's to be expected. After all, human beings are very complex creatures, often behaving one way in one situation and another way when circumstances are different. Still, it can be difficult to know how to make sense of conflicting descriptions of yourself. If one aspect of your hands says you are confident, while another suggests you're shy, should you ignore one? And if so, which one?

The answer is that you should pay attention to both because both are likely to be valid. As you've probably experienced, sometimes a stronger aspect of your personality can help to compensate for a weaker aspect. Your hand merely reflects the fact that you can do this. Even in the case of conflicting information, you will probably notice a trend toward one trait or the other. For example, there may be three indications that you are an outgoing person and only one that you are shy. Thus, in general, you're probably self-assured and comfortable with other people.

Remember, although your hand shape and finger length aren't likely to change that much over time, the same is not true for the lines on your palms. They can change considerably as you make choices and develop your potential. It can be interesting to examine these lines five years from now when you have encountered different experiences and learned new ways of doing things. The changes you've made in the way in which you approach life should be reflected in the map in your hands.

The Map in My Hands

My Hand	What This Says About Me
Shape:	
The Length of My Fingers	
In General:	
My Index Finger:	
My Middle Finger:	
My Ring Finger:	
My Little Finger:	
The Length of My Thumb:	
My Life Line	
Length:	
Direction:	
Strength:	

My Hand	What This Says About Me
My Head Line	
Length:	
Direction:	
Strength:	
My Heart Line	
Length:	
Direction:	
Strength:	
How My Life Line and Head Line Begin	
Separately:	
Entwined:	
With head line below life line:	

3

Numerology

We've Got Your Number!

As you may know, everything in the universe is composed of atoms moving at different rates of speed. Thus, everything in the universe vibrates. We are aware of vibrations that we can hear or feel, but most vibrations are too high or too low for us to detect.

Like everything else, the primary numbers 1 through 9 have vibrations too, ones that are similar to the notes of a musical scale. You have your own unique vibration as well. According to numerology, your vibration was determined at birth by the numbers in your birth date and by the letters (which can be converted into numbers) in the name you were given. Your numerical vibration can harmonize with other vibrations, be in opposition to them, or be unaffected by them.

Numerology is a way of using the numbers in your birth date and name to better understand yourself and to find your place in the world. By knowing your numbers, you can learn to harmonize your vibration with that of the universe and thereby lead a happier and more fulfilling life. Doing a full analysis of your numbers is fairly complicated, so for now we'll just concentrate on the two most important numbers, your life path number and your expression number.

Your Life Path Number

Your birth date contains information about the cycles of your life, the timing of certain events that are likely to happen to you, and the challenges you will need to overcome. But the most important number in your birth date—in fact, your most important number, period—is your life path number. This number tells you the direction you should follow in life, or the path that best suits you. For this reason, it is sometimes also called your destiny number.

If you wish, you can think of your life path as a silent melody that has been playing since the moment you were born. The way you live your life is your attempt to sing that melody. The closer your voice comes to matching the melody, the more "in tune," harmonious, and satisfying your life is likely to be. On the other hand, the more "off key" you are, the more likely you are to feel frustrated and unhappy. Of course, singing a song is a lot easier if you can hear the melody. Your life path number tells you what your melody sounds like.

To find your life path number, simply add all the numbers of your birth date together. Let's take Caitlin Clark's birth date as an example. Caitlin was born on July 22, 1988, or 7/22/1988. $7+2+2+1+9+8+8 = 37$.

Since Caitlin was born before the year 2000, the total is a two-digit number. (Birth date numbers for some people born between January 1, 2000, and January 1, 2005, may total only one digit.) If the total is more than one digit, keep adding the digits together until you get a single-digit number. In Caitlin's case, 3+7 = 10, and 1+0 = 1. Thus, Caitlin's life path number is 1.

Caitlin's younger brother, Kevin, was born August 31, 1995, or 8/31/1995. The numbers in his birth date total 36. 3+6 = 9, so Kevin's life path number is 9.

Now, find your life path number in the same way. Then look below to see what that number tells you about your path through life.

Life Path 1: Leadership

If your life path number is 1, your path in life is to lead. You are a self-starter with the drive, ambition, determination, concentration, and self-confidence to go after what you want and to get it. Although you generally prefer working alone, you have a magnetic personality and are popular with others. Combine that with your originality, bravery, and courage, and it's no wonder that others naturally follow you. On the negative side, you can also be selfish, impatient, and domineering.

Numerologists have noticed that certain colors are frequently associated with specific life paths. Your life path has always been linked with shades of yellow. You may find that wearing yellow increases your determination to succeed. If you don't particularly like yellow, then gold or brown can have a similar effect.

Life Path 2: Cooperation

While number 1's like to "go it alone," your path in life is to work in cooperation with others. Polite, considerate, and diplomatic, you are a valuable addition to any partnership or team. Considering that you are often rather shy, it may come as a surprise to learn that many number 2's become celebrities. Frequently, it's your musical talent that places you in the limelight. However, as a number 2, you need to be careful  that your concern for others' feelings doesn't interfere with your ability to make decisions that are right for you.

If you are like most people with your life path, you probably gravitate toward the color blue. With its soothing and calming effects, this color helps you to increase your own sense of tranquillity and to smooth your relationships with other people.

Life Path 3: Sociability and Entertainment

The world would be a dull, gray place indeed without you! As a number 3, your path in life is to bring joy and a sense of fun and sociability to others. Number

3's are almost always popular, and with good reason. You are optimistic, colorful, creative, imaginative, witty, and love to have a good time. You also tend to be lucky, and no matter what happens, something always seems to turn up for you. On the downside, you can easily become bored and restless. And, while your easy sociability and happy-go-lucky attitude are wonderful qualities, you need to be careful that they don't result in your becoming superficial.

Purple, violet, and mauve are the shades associated with your life path number. These shades help to attract others to you.

Life Path 4: Building Solid Foundations

The number 4 is the most solid and substantial of the numbers. Thus, it makes sense that your life path is to build solid foundations. These can be the foundations of a house, a family, a business, a government, or virtually anything that can benefit from having a secure base. As a number 4, you have all the traits needed to accomplish this—dependability, willingness to work hard, efficiency, practicality, honesty, and resourcefulness. However, you need to guard against becoming too rigid in your thinking.

The color associated with a number 4 life path is

red. Since red gives a person energy and intensity, wearing this color can increase your ability to reach your goals.

Life Path 5: Creating Change

While 4 is the most solid of the numbers, 5 is the least substantial. Because of this, you sometimes have an elusive quality that makes you harder to describe. However, one thing is for sure—almost all number 5's seek a life of freedom and change. Thus, it's not surprising that you are versatile, adaptable, quick-thinking, progressive, and love to travel. The number 5 is also the most potentially creative of the numbers. But the thing that distinguishes you from other people is your skill with words. For this reason, you are often known as the communicators of the world. Your need for change, however, may make it hard for you to stick with a project long enough to finish it. You may also be tempted to take unnecessary risks.

The color orange enhances creativity, cheerfulness, and conversational skills. Therefore, this color is strongly associated with a number 5 life path.

Life Path 6: Seeking Harmony

The number of harmony is 6. Therefore, your life path is to seek and create harmony. Number 6's need a peaceful home life to function best. Loyal, fair, responsible, and capable, you are a good friend and make friends for life. With your basic sense of fairness and balance, you have a talent for helping others resolve conflicts. Most number 6's have a great appreciation for the arts and for things of beauty, and many of you have excellent voices. The major pitfall you need to watch out for is your tendency to interfere in other people's affairs.

Since green is the color of those who are in balance with their surroundings, wearing this color will reinforce your own sense of harmony.

Life Path 7: Individualism

The life path of number 7 individuals is to seek knowledge independently and to learn from their own experience. In many cultures throughout history, 7 has been thought to be a mysterious, magical, or mystical number. Therefore, it makes sense that you are usually very interested in understanding the deeper meaning of life. It also explains why you are more likely than other people to have psychic abilities. You need a fair amount of private time every day to study, think, or just be by yourself, and you function much better when working alone than as part of a team. Although you are an

emotional person, you tend to keep your feelings hidden. As a result, others may think you are cold and arrogant.

The color gray suits your secretive nature and helps you feel protected from the outside world.

Life Path 8: Power and Success

As a number 8, you are driven to succeed in a material sense. As such, you are strong, tough, dynamic, independent, and a hard worker who often enjoys the struggle for power. You determine your goals and then methodically set out to achieve them. As you might imagine, you do particularly well in the business world. Money and material things are important to you, both for their own sakes and as a symbol of your success. Negatively, the effort to succeed can leave you little time for friends and family. And too much emphasis on power and material rewards can make you greedy and overambitious.

Number 8's are often drawn to more somber colors. However, you may find that wearing lighter colors occasionally helps you to relax and "lighten up" a little.

Life Path 9: Humanitarianism

The number 9 contains all the previous numbers within it; thus, it is the most powerful number of all. It stands to reason that this power should be used for the betterment of the world. Therefore, your path in life is to work toward improving life for everyone. Number 9's have the traits that would be expected for this job—you are idealistic, optimistic, compassionate, tolerant, determined, courageous, energetic, creative, and charismatic. Like Number 7's, you may also have psychic abilities. However, if you aren't careful to control all this energy and drive, you may become aggressive and quick-tempered.

Many Number 9's find brown to be a comforting color. Brown is a combination of orange, which helps to increase your creativity and cheerfulness, and black, which lessens your tendency to lose your temper.

If you wish, you can enter the information about your life path number in your own numerology chart on page 85.

Your Expression Number

Like your birth date, your name is also a melody. Each sound, or letter, in your name has a vibration that matches the vibration of a number. The numbers of your name hold the clues to your personality—the traits you were born with, what motivates you, your inner desires, your strengths and weaknesses, and the way in which you interact with other people. However, the most important clue in your name is your expression number—the number that describes how you interact with others.

To find your expression number, you need to change each letter of your name into the corresponding number, then add these numbers together. *Be sure to use your full name.* However, don't include any designations that may follow your name, such as Jr.

The chart below shows the number associated with each letter.

1	2	3	4	5	6	7	8	9
A	B	C	D	E	F	G	H	I
J	K	L	M	N	O	P	Q	R
S	T	U	V	W	X	Y	Z	

Let's use Caitlin's name as an example. Her full name is Caitlin Anne Clark. First, change her letters into the corresponding numbers. Then add these numbers together until you have a one-digit number. (If the total is a three-digit number, add the three digits together. For example, 144 would be added 1+4+4 = 9.)

```
C   A   I   T   L   I   N        A   N   N   E        C   L   A   R   K
3 + 1 + 9 + 2 + 3 + 9 + 5        1 + 5 + 5 + 5        3 + 3 + 1 + 9 + 2   = 66
                                                                 6 + 6 = 12
                                                                 1 + 2 =  3
```

Caitlin's expression number is 3.

You may want to do each of your names separately, since this is a good way to check your addition. If you haven't made any mistakes, adding the numbers of each name together should give you the same expression number you got by adding your whole name at once. In Caitlin's case:

```
C   A   I   T   L   I   N          A   N   N   E          C   L   A   R   K
3 + 1 + 9 + 2 + 3 + 9 + 5 = 32     1 + 5 + 5 + 5 = 16      3 + 3 + 1 + 9 + 2 = 18
          3 + 2 = 5                   1 + 6 = 7                   1 + 8 = 9
```

When you add Caitlin's names together, you get 5 + 7 + 9 = 21. 2 + 1 = 3.

For some people, the name they use now may not be the name they were given at birth. This happens most often when a woman takes her husband's last name upon getting married. But it also occurs when children are adopted.

The name you were given when you were born has the strongest influence on you, even if you don't know what that name is. But any other name you are known by can affect the kind of opportunities and experiences you attract. In fact, some people actually change the spelling of their name, or change their name altogether, in an attempt to improve the opportunities that come their way. Therefore, if you are adopted and you know your original name, use that name in figuring out your expression number. If not, use your adopted name.

Now that you've found your expression number, let's see what it tells you about the way in which you interact with other people. Incidentally, since others see this part of you every time they interact with you, you may want to ask your friends how well they think your expression number describes you.

Expression Number 1

You interact with others in a forceful, original, daring, creative, and assertive manner. You like to take charge and to lead others, and you're happiest when you are the boss or are free to carry out your own ideas. Not surprisingly, you don't like having to follow someone else's orders.

Expression Number 2

Known for your friendliness and tact, you strive for cooperative relationships with others. You are patient, cope well with details, and are willing to work behind the scenes. Although somewhat shy, you attract people to you. You may find it hard to make decisions or to take a stand, however.

Expression Number 3

You are cheerful, outgoing, animated, expressive, imaginative, witty, and creative in your interactions with others. You need a lively social life, and your ability to create fun and laughter makes you popular with others. However, you often get bored quickly and may have difficulty finishing what you've started.

Expression Number 4

You are sincere, honest, practical, and logical in your relationships with other people. You also have a great deal of self-discipline and are a hard worker. You tend to be conservative and stubborn, however, and need to take care that you don't become rigid in your way of doing things.

Expression Number 5

You are adaptable, adventuresome, entertaining, and versatile in interacting with others. These traits plus your skill at communicating make you popular and at ease with many different types of people. However, to be comfortable, you need a great deal of freedom in your relationships.

Expression Number 6

You seek harmony and love in your relationships with others, offering understanding, stability, trust, loyalty, and a willingness to shoulder responsibilities. You function best when you have a peaceful home life. Take care not to meddle in others' affairs, however.

Expression Number 7

You tend to be quiet, aloof, and secretive in relating to other people. You are an individualist and don't like being taught by others. It takes you a while to get close to people, and even then, you need to have time by yourself to think and to dream. But be careful that your daydreams don't replace real life.

Expression Number 8

Success-oriented, you are aggressive, practical, organized, self-assured, efficient, and direct in your relationships to others. When you are at your best, you can also be quite generous. However, you need to be careful that your desire for wealth and power does not make you greedy and power hungry.

Expression Number 9

You are compassionate, idealistic, and broad-minded in your interactions with others. You feel a connection with all human beings, regardless of their race, ethnic group, religion, or gender, and want to work with others to improve life for all. You can be a charismatic, although sometimes impractical, leader.

This is a good time to add the information about your expression number to your own numerology chart.

How Do Your Numbers Fit Together?

In general, odd numbers are harmonious with other odd numbers, while even numbers are harmonious with other even numbers. If your life path and expression numbers are harmonious, your personality is well-suited for the path in life that is best for you. If they are not, you'll have to learn to make some adjustments.

For example, if your life path number is 7, your destiny is to seek knowledge independently, but if your expression number is 2, you prefer to work cooperatively with others. As you can see, it's hard to do both these things at the same time. In this case, finding your way may be more difficult for you than for some others. However, it helps to know what the problem is. That way, you can figure out how best to make your life work for you.

Now that you've had a chance to see what your numbers say about you, what do you think about this information? In reading about their life path, many people recognize it as the direction they were trying to go in anyway. Is this true for you as well, or does your life path seem wrong for you? Remember, no one says that you *have* to follow that path. The choice of how you live your life is up to you.

What about the way your numbers say you interact with others? Does that seem to fit or not? As mentioned earlier, you can not only check the description of your expression number against the way you think you interact with others, but you can ask your friends for their opinion as well. After all, they've probably already "got your number."

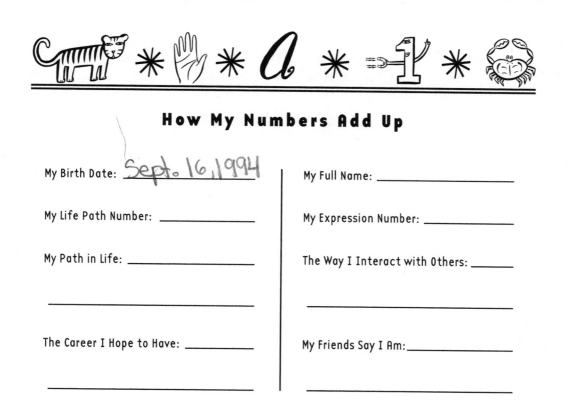

How My Numbers Add Up

My Birth Date: _Sept. 16, 1994_

My Life Path Number: _____

My Path in Life: _____

_____

The Career I Hope to Have: _____

_____

My Full Name: _____

My Expression Number: _____

The Way I Interact with Others: _____

_____

My Friends Say I Am: _____

_____

How My Numbers Fit Together:

4

Chinese Horoscopes

The Animal That Hides in Your Heart

rom his throne in the sky, the Jade Emperor looked down at the earth. "Since the beginning of time, I have ruled all that exists in the heavens and beyond," he said to his chief counselor. "But I have never been to earth. Tell me of the creatures who live there. What do they look like and how do they sound? In what manner do they help mankind?"

The chief counselor replied that the creatures of the earth were too many to count. "Do you wish to know about all of them?" he asked.

"No," said the Jade Emperor. "Choose the twelve most interesting and bring them to me. That will suffice."

The chief counselor hurried to earth and summoned the twelve animals he knew best. "You are to appear before the Jade Emperor tomorrow morning," he told the rat, the cat, the ox, the dog, the tiger, the sheep, the horse, the snake, the rooster, the dragon, the rabbit, and the monkey.

The twelve animals were all very excited. But the cat, who had a tendency to oversleep, worried that he might not awaken in time. "Be sure to call me at the first light of dawn," the cat said to his best friend, the rat. And the rat promised to do so.

But during the night, the rat remembered how beautiful the cat was and how unattractive he looked by comparison. So, when dawn broke, the rat slipped quietly past his friend and made his way to the heavenly throne, leaving the cat fast asleep.

The Jade Emperor looked with pleasure at the animals before him. "But why are there only eleven?" he asked the chief counselor. "I asked you to bring me twelve."

Fearing the Jade Emperor's anger, the chief counselor decided not to wait for the cat. Quickly, he sped back to earth and grabbed the first animal he saw—a pig.

The Jade Emperor was so impressed with the animals before him that he promised to name a year for each of them. Just then, the cat dashed up to the throne and begged the Jade Emperor to include him. "You are too late," the Jade Emperor said. "The twelve years have already been awarded to others." Realizing that his friend had tricked him, the cat vowed to kill the rat. And to this day, the cat remains the sworn enemy of the rat.

This is how the rat, ox, tiger, rabbit, dragon, snake, horse, sheep, monkey, rooster, dog, and pig each came to be associated with a year in the Chinese calendar. The Chinese believe that the animal that rules the year of your birth has a powerful influence on your life and your personality. Thus, this is the animal "that hides in your heart." It is the most important aspect of your Chinese astrological horoscope.

Of course, there is much more to Chinese astrology than the animal traits associated with your birth year. Otherwise, almost everyone in your grade at school would have the same personality as you do—and that certainly isn't the case! But the animal that rules your year is definitely the best place to start. Later, we'll also look at your ascendant—the shadow animal that's with you always.

Your Animal Year

Finding Your Animal Year

To find out which animal rules your birth year, you need to know your birth year according to the Chinese calendar. Unlike the Western solar calendar, which is based on the orbit of the earth around the sun, the Chinese lunar calendar is based on the orbit of the moon around the earth. Instead of months, the lunar year is divided into moons. Each lunar year has 12 moons and each moon lasts just over 29 days. This means that the lunar year is always a little shorter (353 to 355 days) than the solar year (364 1/4 days). To make the two calendars coincide, an extra month is added to the lunar calendar about every three years.

The Chinese lunar year also starts at a different time of the year than the

Western solar year. While the solar year begins on January 1, the lunar year starts sometime between late January and mid-February, depending on the year.

To determine your lunar birth year, find your birth date on the chart on pages 112–16. If you were born anytime between March 1 and December 31, your Western birth year and Chinese birth year are the same. But if your birthday falls in January or February, you need to examine the chart carefully, because you may belong to the previous animal year. Once you've found your birth year, look to the right to find the animal that rules your year. The chart goes back far enough that you should be able to find your parents' and grandparents' animal years too, if you wish.

Triangles of Affinity

Before reading about your animal, it's a good idea to know which animals have characteristics in common. This will help you understand why you are compatible with some people but not with others. Learning these similarities can also help you remember the traits of each animal.

Just as Western astrology groups signs according to the element—fire, air, water, or earth—associated with them, Chinese astrology also divides the animals into four groups of three animals each. Animals within each group share important personality traits and therefore get along well with each other; thus, these animals form a triangle of affinity.

The first triangle of affinity is composed of the Rat, the Dragon, and the

Monkey. People born in the years ruled by these animals are the doers of the world. Energetic and ambitious self-starters, they are full of innovative ideas and eager to put them into action. However, if hindered in carrying out their plans or forced to be inactive, they can be restless and quick-tempered.

The Ox, the Snake, and the Rooster make up the second triangle of affinity.

Those born in these years are steady, purposeful, dedicated people who succeed by sheer determination, careful planning, and perseverance. They tend to be fixed in their views and deliberate in their actions. They are also the most intellectual and listen more to their heads than to their hearts.

The animals that compose the third triangle of affinity—the Tiger, the Horse, and the Dog—are the great communicators and servers of mankind. People born in the years ruled by these animals are extroverted, honest, open, idealistic, and high-spirited, and establish strong relationships with others. Obtaining justice and fairness for everyone is important to them.

The fourth triangle of affinity is made up of the Rabbit, the Sheep, and the Pig. These are the artistic and emotional animals of Chinese astrology. Thus, people born in these years are compassionate, intuitive, artistically talented, and attracted to things of beauty. They have calmer personalities than do those born in other years and tend to rely on others for leadership.

Circle of Conflict

Just as people who are born in some years are likely to get along, those born in other years are likely to experience conflict. In the Chinese circle of conflict, people born in the years ruled by animals who are directly opposite each other are likely to clash.

Now that you know something about the relationships between the twelve animal signs, let's take a look at the animal that hides in *your* heart. To help

you remember this information, you may want to write down key words describing your animal in your animal profile on pages 117–18. This will also be helpful later when you're ready to combine the information about your animal year and your ascendant. If you wish, you can also add the animals that form your triangle of affinity and the animal opposite you on the circle of conflict.

The Rat

If you were born in the year of the Rat, you are intelligent and quick to take advantage of any opportunity, particularly when there's money to be made. Rats have a sharp business sense and are hardworking, efficient, organized, practical, and innovative. As a result, you usually do quite well financially. Yet there's nothing underhanded in the way you get ahead, for despite your strong will and ambition, you treat others fairly.

As a typically levelheaded Rat, you thrive on challenges and are very handy to have around in times of crisis. However, you're even better at avoiding these situations in the first place. With your intuition, ability to plan ahead, strong sense of self-preservation, and skill at watching your back, you rarely get caught off guard.

Fortunately, Rats are well aware that life is not all business. A fun-loving person, you're right at home at parties and other large social events. And your open, friendly, and charming personality makes you easy to get along with. You have a very sentimental side as well, and are deeply attached to your friends and family. However, while Rats enjoy the company of others, you also value your privacy and guard it well.

On the downside, it takes a lot to part you from your money, and if you're not careful, you can become stingy or even a tad greedy. You also run the risk of being selfish, stubborn, or overambitious. With your deep need to feel secure, you are likely to be overly anxious when you think your security is threatened.

You are most compatible with people born in the years of the Dragon and the Monkey, the other two signs in your triangle of affinity. On the other hand, you may have serious conflicts with people born in the year of the Horse. As your direct opposite, they are much too independent and changeable for you. You're also not likely to be crazy about the Rooster, who can be as competitive and critical as you, or the Sheep, whose willingness to spend money freely makes you nervous.

The Ox

As a person born in the year of the Ox, you are calm, dependable, steady, logical, and methodical. Basically conservative, you respect traditions and dislike taking risks. You are also somewhat of an introvert and need peace and quiet to work out your ideas and plans. However, once you've made a decision, you  stick to it. In fact, you are noted for your ability to persevere, even in the most difficult circumstances.

As a friend, you are truthful, honest, fair-minded, charitable, patient, sincere, and always keep your word—so it's no wonder that you are well-liked by others. And, as long as you feel secure, you can be very sociable. However, on the rare occasions when you lose your temper, it's an event that others are unlikely to forget.

Although not ordinarily a leader, in times of chaos it is often the Ox who steps forward to save the day. Your presence of mind, determination, and refusal to be intimidated in these situations allow you to take charge and restore order.

While the ability to stick to your decisions is admirable, you need to be careful that you don't become stubborn, inflexible, and too set in your opinions. You also have a tendency to hold grudges for much too long.

You are most compatible with those born in the years of the Snake and the Rooster, the other signs in your triangle of affinity. In contrast, the Tiger is too adventurous, the Horse is too independent, and the Monkey is too scheming for you to be comfortable with. But your greatest difficulties are likely to be with your direct opposite, the Sheep.

The Tiger

Those of you born in the year of the Tiger often seem larger than life. Always excited by a challenge, you have an incredible gusto for life and throw yourself wholeheartedly into everything you do. Powerful, daring, colorful, rebellious,

exciting, courageous, optimistic, and determined, you're a natural leader who commands respect. Besides being a stimulating person to be around, others are drawn to you because of your sincere, affectionate, generous, warm, loyal, and sympathetic nature. And if that weren't enough, you have a great sense of humor.

Material rewards and security don't interest you. Although you can be impulsive, unpredictable, and reckless, you nevertheless have the drive to finish projects that you start and to reach goals that are important to you. But most of all, you trust in your own charisma and good luck to bring you success.

Unfortunately, the Tiger's more negative traits can be just as impressive. To put it bluntly, you often have a giant ego. You can be very stubborn and self-centered when you don't get your way, and failure or loss of face can be difficult for you to handle. Strangely, you have a tendency to be too suspicious in some situations and overly trusting in others. Perhaps your worst fault, however, is that you will often do anything to get revenge when you feel you've been crossed.

As you would expect, you get along best with others in your triangle of affinity, the Horse and the Dog. You're least compatible with your opposite sign, the Monkey. Both you and the Monkey are very competitive and are very sore losers—which can be a disastrous combination. It's not a great idea for you to tangle with the Ox either, for this is one fight you may not win. You are too aggressive for the Rabbit, and you and the Snake are too suspicious of each other to become friends.

The Rabbit

In Chinese mythology, the Rabbit is the symbol of a long life. Therefore, people born in the year ruled by this animal are considered very fortunate. You have been blessed with many admirable traits as well, including your charm, elegance, graciousness, kindness, and generosity. With your  tranquil, reserved nature, you are happiest in peaceful environments. You have no interest in being in the limelight, and you work hard at avoiding confrontations or unpleasantness of any kind.

If you are like most Rabbits, you have good judgment, a sharp business sense, and strong negotiating skills—and, on top of this, you tend to be lucky when it comes to money. In addition to your business sense, you also have a good imagination and a strongly artistic side. You love material comforts, and with your excellent taste and sensitivity to beauty, you easily create a beautiful and luxurious lifestyle.

As you might guess, Rabbits do not do well in competitive or aggressive environments. Nor do you feel comfortable in unpredictable or risky situations. But anyone who mistakes this for weakness is in for a surprise. You are extremely strong-willed and self-confident, and can be quite persevering when you want something.

On the other hand, you can often be too cautious for your own good, and may lose out on promising opportunities as a result. You can also be self-indulgent and have a tendency to put yourself first.

Your closest relationships are likely to be with the Sheep and the Pig, the other animals in your triangle of affinity. However, your opposite, the vain and critical Rooster, is definitely not your cup of tea. And you're likely to be equally unimpressed with the Tiger and the Horse.

The Dragon

With your majestic, aristocratic, and charismatic personality, it's probably easy for people to identify you as someone born in the year of the Dragon. A bit of a show-off, you love being the center of attention and have no trouble attracting the spotlight. Your boundless energy, enthusiasm for life, and interest in the world around you make you an exciting person to be around. Besides being lively company, you are generous, loyal, open with your feelings, and quick to forgive. Thus, others consider themselves fortunate to know you.

Decisive, frank, and capable, you enjoy being in charge and are a natural leader. Because you are generally fair in your dealings with others and set high standards for yourself as well as for them, you gain respect effortlessly. And those in trouble or in need can always count on you for help.

In Chinese astrology, the Dragon is the sign of wealth and power. Therefore, you have the potential to achieve great success. And with your talents, unlimited energy, and willingness to exhaust all possibilities before admitting failure, you're likely to rise to the top in any situation.

Like the Tiger, however, your weaknesses can be as big as your strengths. One of your major problems is your tendency to let your pride slip into arrogance. You may even come to feel that you are better than others and do not need to follow the rules that govern them. Your pride can also make it difficult for you to ask for help, even when you sorely need it. In addition to being too proud, you can also be too demanding of others and too willing to try to intimidate those who dare to oppose you.

Your best relationships are with the Rat and the Monkey, the others in your triangle of affinity. The Dog, your direct opposite, is the most difficult for you. Dogs are too clear-eyed to be impressed by your charismatic personality and you don't appreciate being analyzed by them. Also, the fair-minded Dog is not likely to let you get away with any attempt to place yourself above others.

The Snake

People born in the year of the Snake are the puzzles of the Chinese zodiac. A secretive person, you treasure your privacy and rarely betray your true feelings. In times of crisis, your ability to keep your cool, assess the situation, and act decisively gives you a special strength. You seem to have been born with a certain wisdom, and you trust your own instincts and judgment completely.

As the most intense sign of the Chinese cycle, the Snake has a magnetic appeal. Graceful, elegant, well-mannered, and soft-spoken, you're attracted to the finer things in life. Fortunately, with your shrewd business sense, you can afford them. You are also the deepest thinker of all the signs, and you love stimulating debate and interesting conversation. You place great value on your friendships and are extremely caring and protective toward those who are important to you. In fact, any attempt to hurt someone you care about is guaranteed to result in quick retaliation from you. Although you resist accepting advice, you are good at helping others. And your fabulous sense of humor can lighten any situation.

It's a rare Snake who isn't ambitious for power and authority. As one of the most persistent signs of the Chinese zodiac, you are very likely to achieve this goal. And, once you have power in your hands, you're not likely to let it go. One way or another, your life is highly unlikely to be dull. In fact, with your love of excitement and intrigue, it may even be downright dangerous.

Unfortunately, in your effort to gain power, you can sometimes be ruthless and willing to do anything to succeed. And heaven help those who break a promise to you. If it takes years, you'll usually manage to settle the score. You can also be very possessive and demanding of others.

Your best friends are likely to be the others in your triangle of affinity, the Ox and the Rooster. In contrast, you probably won't care much for the Tiger, the Horse, and the Monkey. The most serious clashes, however, will occur between you and those born in the year of the Pig, your opposite sign.

The Horse

Independent, unpredictable, nonconformist, impetuous, high-spirited, and adventurous are only some of the words that describe those born in the year of the Horse. Almost everything about you seems quick, from your swift, graceful physical movements and rapid speech to your lively mind and ability to respond immediately to changing situations. With your charm, optimistic self-assurance, and eloquent speaking ability, you are remarkably persuasive and have the potential to be an inspiring leader. Others confide in you because they sense that you are genuinely interested in them. And they value you as a friend because of your cheerfulness, honesty, and warmth. You're also willing to allow others the same independence that you want for yourself, and thus your relationships are free of possessiveness and jealousy.

You are noted for your ability to handle money and can, if you wish, become wealthy. However, you're not interested in security. Far more important to you is a stimulating and challenging job that does not trap you in a rigid schedule. You are inspired by ideas and tend to act on them immediately. When something has caught your interest, you're willing to work long, hard hours. And you're particularly good at finding easy, clever solutions to any problem.

However, your changeable nature can also cause difficulties for you and those around you. For example, you sometimes neglect to finish one thing before moving on to something else. You also have a tendency to expect others to rush into things simply because you want them to. And you can be hot-tempered, headstrong, impulsive, and childish when you don't get your way.

The Tiger and the Dog, the others in your triangle of affinity, are likely to be your best friends. On the other hand, you are too inconsistent for the Ox and the Rabbit, and you have little in common with the Snake. However, your most difficult relationships are likely to be with your direct opposite, the Rat. You are independent, carefree, and resist being restricted, so the last person you need is the clannish, persistent, and possessive Rat.

The Sheep

If you were born in the year of the Sheep, you are a gentle, sensitive, dreamy romantic. You go out of your way to avoid conflict and are distressed if you've accidentally hurt someone or have let a friend down. You have a compassionate and forgiving nature, and those who are down and out can always turn to you for help.

A deeply emotional person, you are moved by things of beauty, such as a painting, a piece of music, or a flower in bloom. Often, you have considerable artistic talent. On the other hand, you dislike rigid schedules and have trouble tolerating too much discipline. Not only do you resist being tied to a routine, but you may also have trouble staying in one place. In fact, it's not uncommon for the Sheep to just take off one day to see the world.

The Chinese believe that good luck follows those born in your year because of your peaceful nature and kind heart. Therefore, whatever happens, you'll always have the things you need to survive—food, a place to live, and clothing. Fortune smiles on you in other ways as well. Inevitably, when everything is at its bleakest, something or someone always turns up to rescue you.

Unfortunately, your sensitive nature can be overcome by negative emotions as easily as positive ones, and you may often feel depressed, worried, or full of self-pity. Competition, pressure, and unexpected situations throw you for a loop. You can have difficulty making decisions and need to guard against merely floating through life.

As you might expect, you get along best with those born in the year of the Rabbit and the Pig, for they share your sensitivity and artistic tastes. On the other hand, the Rat, the Dog, the Rooster, and your opposite sign, the Ox, are not good choices for you.

The Monkey

Clever, inventive, quick-witted, and a talented improviser, the Monkey is the most ingenious of the Chinese cycle. It takes you only a few moments to size up an opportunity and figure out how to take advantage of it. A remarkably quick study, you're able to solve difficult problems with ease. In fact, there is virtually nothing you can't do if you put your mind to it!

Your skill at manipulating others is just as impressive as your other talents. Charming, cunning, and extremely persuasive, you could talk the shirt off someone's back and they'd probably thank you for helping them to feel cooler. This doesn't mean that you are dishonest, but one way or another, you always manage to come out ahead in any deal.

Part of your skill with others is that you are extremely social and know how to make people like you. You are warm, spontaneous, sparkling, humorous, and have a love of life that is contagious. You are also willing to work hard, as long as there is something in it for you. Besides admiring you for your many abilities, others come to rely on your versatility and resourcefulness and soon find it hard to do without you.

Still, your cunning and the fact that you seem to get what you want effortlessly often make people suspicious of you. In turn, you're not a very trusting person yourself. Thus, while you may be very popular, you tend to be truly close to only a few people.

Perhaps because you can so easily get people to do what you want, you may not have as much respect for others as you should. And your extreme competitiveness can sometimes make you jealous of others' success.

Your best friends are likely to be the Rat and the Dragon, the others in your triangle of affinity. On the other hand, the Ox is too slow for your taste, and the Snake may give you a run for your money. But you're least likely to get along with your opposite sign, the Tiger.

The Rooster

If you were born in the year of the Rooster, you're likely to evoke strong reactions from other people. In fact, they're usually very attracted to you or go out of their way to avoid you. But one thing's for sure—they can't help but notice you. You love being the center of attention and work hard to get there. Not that attracting the spotlight is difficult for you. With your good looks, fine clothes, and dignified bearing, you cut an imposing figure. Cheerful, amusing, witty, intelligent, and a sparkling conversationalist, you're a born performer and a natural for life in the public eye. It's just that sometimes your very elevated opinion of yourself can be a bit much.

Ironically, what others often don't understand is that all this show is as much to convince yourself as it is to impress them. For, underneath, you tend to feel vulnerable and not all that confident. This is too bad, because you have many admirable traits, including a good heart and a strong conscience. Although your sharp criticism can be difficult to take, you mean well and you're always willing to pitch in and help others.

At heart, the typical Rooster is a perfectionist. You are a hard worker and a skilled manager, with a careful eye for detail. You're also particularly good at handling money. Although you are likely to be successful in life, you'll have to work for it, since things will not fall effortlessly into your lap.

Your super-blunt tongue and often brutally honest criticism can be hard for many people to deal with, even if you are usually right. And the people you help may feel you are taking over their lives in your attempt to aid them. If you could tone down a bit, you might find that your relationships with others would be smoother.

Those most likely to appreciate you are the Ox and the Snake, the others in your triangle of affinity. The Rat and the Sheep are not particularly good friends for you, however. Nor are you likely to do well with another Rooster. Your worst relationship is likely to be with your opposite sign, the sensitive Rabbit, who will dislike your lack of tact and your tendency to provoke arguments.

The Dog

The humanitarian Dog is the symbol of justice, and those born in the year of the Dog are always ready to fight for a worthy cause or defend those treated unfairly. You are honest, idealistic, intelligent, straightforward, and deeply loyal to your friends, and you feel it is your duty to protect others, particularly those close to you. You also have the ability to see through people—and size up their mo-  tives—very clearly. Thus, not much escapes your notice. Unprejudiced and open-minded, you want to know all the facts before you reach a decision, but once you have made up your mind, you don't often change it.

Although you are somewhat of an introvert, your fearlessness, integrity, and the trust you inspire in others can land you in positions of leadership. And, while you aren't likely to seek out the job of leader, you'll do it effectively.

Perhaps because you see things so clearly, you're likely to have a pessimistic streak, often worrying unnecessarily and expecting problems at every turn. Yet you are hardly glum or depressing to be around. On the contrary, the Dog may be the most genuinely likable of all the signs. You are warm, friendly, loyal, attractive, lively, fair, reasonable, modest, and always willing to do your share. What more could anyone want in a friend? Still, most people born in the year of the Dog are a bit defensive and do not trust others quickly. You need a little time to warm up to someone, but others generally feel that it's well worth the wait.

You have few negative traits. Perhaps the most prominent are your lack of patience and your tendency to snap at people who irritate you. You also need to realize that you can't take responsibility for righting *all* the wrongs of the world.

You relate most comfortably with the Horse and the Tiger, the other signs in your triangle of affinity. In contrast, you probably won't particularly like the Sheep. Those born in the year of the Dragon are the worst possibility for you, however. You see through their overconfidence and never quite trust them.

The Pig

As someone born in the year of the Pig, you are the original "good guy" of the Chinese zodiac. Innocent and often naive, you are very trusting. You hate fighting and see no reason why everyone can't get along—and you go out of

your way to try to make interactions pleasanter for everyone. Because you look for the best in people, you
often find it. As an honest, gallant, generous,
kind, understanding person with a heart of gold,
you are eagerly sought after by those looking for a
good friend. You also enjoy all kinds of social gath-
erings and definitely appreciate the good things
in life.

   Although you are hardworking, Pigs are not particularly ambitious. Usually, you have little interest in positions of power and instead prefer the com-
panionship of working as part of a team. But the fact that you are an
accommodating person doesn't mean that others can push you around. When
you feel someone has gone too far, you are capable of responding savagely and
can become a fierce enemy.

   Your main failing is that you are too trusting and can be at the mercy of
those willing to take advantage of you. You also may have as much trouble saying no to yourself as to others. Sometimes, you can enjoy the good life a little
too much, and need to develop some self-restraint if you want to avoid financial or health problems.

   As you might expect, you get along famously with the others in your triangle of affinity, the Rabbit and the Sheep, for both share your need for harmony
and peace. However, watch out for your opposite sign, the Snake, as well as the
Monkey. They're both a little too crafty for you to handle.

Your Ascendant

In addition to the animal that rules your year of birth, you have another animal that influences you as well. This is your ascendant, the animal that rules the hour you were born. Your Chinese ascendant can be compared to your shadow, or the other side of your personality. Sometimes, your shadow is even longer than you are, while at other times, you can hardly see it. But, no matter how noticeable it is, your shadow—and your shadow animal—are always part of you.

Your ascendant is one of the main reasons your personality may be different from that of someone else who was born in your year. It also has a lot to do with determining the people you are compatible with, as well as those you don't like very much. *Two people usually feel a strong attraction to each other when the animal ascendant of one is the same as the animal year of the other.* This is true even when the two people would not ordinarily be compatible in terms of their animal years.

Similarly, you may find that you don't get along well at all with someone whose animal ascendant is directly opposite your animal year on the circle of conflict. This can be true even if your animal years are very harmonious.

Finding Your Ascendant

To find your ascendant, you need to know the hour of your birth. Often, the time you were born is included on your birth certificate, so look there first. If your birth time is not given, ask your parents or grandparents—one of them is likely to remember. Remember, you don't need to know the exact time, just the hour.

If your birth hour is in Daylight Savings Time, be sure to change it into Standard Time by subtracting an hour. However, you don't have to change your birth time into Eastern Standard Time, the way you did when finding your ascendant in chapter one.

Now look at the chart on page 116. It will tell you what animal rules your time of birth. This chart works for everyone, regardless of the place or the time of year you were born. The only problem you may have is if you were born at exactly 1:00, 3:00, 5:00, 7:00, 9:00, or 11:00. In that case, you're probably confused as to which animal you fall under, the one before the hour or the one after the hour. Although very few people are born *exactly* on the hour, this may be the closest you can get to your birth time. If so, read the descriptions of both animals and see which you think fits you best. You can also ask your parents for their opinion.

Now add the key words that describe your ascendant to your animal profile.

Combining Your Animal Year and Ascendant

If your animal year and your ascendant are the same, it's easy to combine them—just credit yourself with a double dose of the same traits. It can also be relatively simple to figure out how the two combine if they are similar in some ways. The difficulty arises when your animal year and ascendant are very different, particularly if they are direct opposites. In that case, each may modify the other, or you may find that you are more like your animal year at some times and more like your ascendant at others. There is also a third possibility, in which the stronger animal sign overpowers the less forceful—for example, if your Rabbit year takes a backseat to your more powerful Dragon ascendant. Even in that case, however, you never lose the Rabbit within you. It's just not as obvious.

If you're still stumped about all this, sit down for a minute and think about yourself. Which traits of your animal year do you recognize in your personality? Which traits of your ascendant do you think are part of you? The two parts don't have to fit together perfectly, you know. People are complex creatures, and that includes you.

The important thing is whether you feel your Chinese horoscope has helped you to understand yourself better. If so, then it's served its purpose.

Animal Years

Lunar Year	Animal
February 5, 1924 to January 24, 1925	Rat
January 25, 1925 to February 12, 1926	Ox
February 13, 1926 to February 1, 1927	Tiger
February 2, 1927 to January 22, 1928	Rabbit
January 23, 1928 to February 9, 1929	Dragon
February 10, 1929 to January 29, 1930	Snake
January 30, 1930 to February 16, 1931	Horse
February 17, 1931 to February 5, 1932	Sheep

Lunar Year	Animal
February 6, 1932 to January 25, 1933	Monkey
January 26, 1933 to February 13, 1934	Rooster
February 14, 1934 to February 3, 1935	Dog
February 4, 1935 to January 23, 1936	Pig
January 24, 1936 to February 10, 1937	Rat
February 11, 1937 to January 30, 1938	Ox
January 31, 1938 to February 18, 1939	Tiger
February 19, 1939 to February 7, 1940	Rabbit
February 8, 1940 to January 26, 1941	Dragon
January 27, 1941 to February 14, 1942	Snake
February 15, 1942 to February 4, 1943	Horse
February 5, 1943 to January 24, 1944	Sheep
January 25, 1944 to February 12, 1945	Monkey
February 13, 1945 to February 1, 1946	Rooster
February 2, 1946 to January 21, 1947	Dog
January 22, 1947 to February 9, 1948	Pig
February 10, 1948 to January 28, 1949	Rat
January 29, 1949 to February 16, 1950	Ox
February 17, 1950 to February 5, 1951	Tiger
February 6, 1951 to January 26, 1952	Rabbit
January 27, 1952 to February 13, 1953	Dragon
February 14, 1953 to February 2, 1954	Snake

Lunar Year	Animal
February 3, 1954 to January 23, 1955	Horse
January 24, 1955 to February 11, 1956	Sheep
February 12, 1956 to January 30, 1957	Monkey
January 31, 1957 to February 17, 1958	Rooster
February 18, 1958 to February 7, 1959	Dog
February 8, 1959 to January 27, 1960	Pig
January 28, 1960 to February 14, 1961	Rat
February 15, 1961 to February 4, 1962	Ox
February 5, 1962 to January 24, 1963	Tiger
January 25, 1963 to February 12, 1964	Rabbit
February 13, 1964 to February 1, 1965	Dragon
February 2, 1965 to January 20, 1966	Snake
January 21, 1966 to February 8, 1967	Horse
February 9, 1967 to January 29, 1968	Sheep
January 30, 1968 to February 16, 1969	Monkey
February 17, 1969 to February 5, 1970	Rooster
February 6, 1970 to January 26, 1971	Dog
January 27, 1971 to February 15, 1972	Pig
February 16, 1972 to February 2, 1973	Rat
February 3, 1973 to January 22, 1974	Ox
January 23, 1974 to February 10, 1975	Tiger
February 11, 1975 to January 30, 1976	Rabbit

Lunar Year	Animal
January 31, 1976 to February 17, 1977	Dragon
February 18, 1977 to February 6, 1978	Snake
February 7, 1978 to January 27, 1979	Horse
January 28, 1979 to February 15, 1980	Sheep
February 16, 1980 to February 4, 1981	Monkey
February 5, 1981 to January 24, 1982	Rooster
January 25, 1982 to February 12, 1983	Dog
February 13, 1983 to February 1, 1984	Pig
February 2, 1984 to February 19, 1985	Rat
February 20, 1985 to February 8, 1986	Ox
February 9, 1986 to January 28, 1987	Tiger
January 29, 1987 to February 16, 1988	Rabbit
February 17, 1988 to February 5, 1989	Dragon
February 6, 1989 to January 26, 1990	Snake
January 27, 1990 to February 14, 1991	Horse
February 15, 1991 to February 3, 1992	Sheep
February 4, 1992 to January 22, 1993	Monkey
January 23, 1993 to February 9, 1994	Rooster
February 10, 1994 to January 30, 1995	Dog
January 31, 1995 to February 18, 1996	Pig
February 19, 1996 to February 6, 1997	Rat
February 7, 1997 to January 27, 1998	Ox

Lunar Year	Animal
January 28, 1998 to February 15, 1999	Tiger
February 16, 1999 to February 4, 2000	Rabbit
February 5, 2000 to January 23, 2001	Dragon
January 24, 2001 to February 11, 2002	Snake
February 12, 2002 to January 31, 2003	Horse
February 1, 2003 to January 21, 2004	Sheep
January 22, 2004 to February 8, 2005	Monkey
February 9, 2005 to January 28, 2006	Rooster
January 29, 2006 to February 17, 2007	Dog
February 18, 2007 to February 6, 2008	Pig

Ascendants

Hours	Ascendant
11:00 P.M. to 1:00 A.M.	Rat
1:00 A.M. to 3:00 A.M.	Ox
3:00 A.M. to 5:00 A.M.	Tiger
5:00 A.M. to 7:00 A.M.	Rabbit
7:00 A.M. to 9:00 A.M.	Dragon
9:00 A.M. to 11:00 A.M.	Snake
11:00 A.M. to 1:00 P.M.	Horse
1:00 P.M. to 3:00 P.M.	Sheep
3:00 P.M. to 5:00 P.M.	Monkey
5:00 P.M. to 7:00 P.M.	Rooster
7:00 P.M. to 9:00 P.M.	Dog
9:00 P.M. to 11:00 P.M.	Pig

My Animal Profile

Name: _____

Birth Date: _____

Birth Time: _____

The Animal That Hides in My Heart	**My Shadow Animal (My Ascendant)**	**A Picture of Me**
My Animal Year: _____ Traits:	My Animal Hour: _____ Traits:	How My Animal Traits Combine: _____

Animals I Get Along with
(My Triangle of Affinity and My Ascendant)

Animal I Conflict with
(My Opposite on the Circle of Conflict)

5

Handwriting Analysis

A Self-Portrait in Disguise

andwriting analysis gives you information about yourself that none of the other systems in this book can. If you think about it, all the others are based primarily on things that are out of your control. For example, solar astrology, Chinese horoscopes, and numerology rely on when you were born or the name you were given, while palm reading depends on the physical features of your hand. In contrast, handwriting analysis is a way of learning about yourself by looking at *what you do.*

Although you may not know it, every time you write something in script, you are painting a portrait of yourself. By using certain clues, a good detective can look at this self-portrait and tell a lot about you.

Handwriting analysis is different in another way as well. Instead of focusing on the traits you were born with, handwriting analysis explores *who you are right now*. Most people's personalities change as they grow and develop. As a result, the way in which they do things usually changes as well. Since your handwriting is something you do, it's a reflection of the changes in your personality over time.

If you'd like to know more about who you are at this point in your life, handwriting analysis is a good way to find out. It's also an easy way to learn more about other people, since all you need are handwriting samples and a few other simple things.

What You'll Need

To get a good handwriting sample and find the clues in it, you'll need the following things:

- A sheet of regular-size (8½ by 11 inches), unlined paper (For reasons we'll talk about later, a small sheet of paper or one with lines is not appropriate.)
- A sheet of thin tracing paper, about the same size as the unlined paper above
- A ballpoint pen
- A pencil
- A ruler

Your Handwriting Sample

Using a ballpoint pen, write the following three lines on a clean sheet of regular-size, unlined paper and sign your name underneath.

This is the way I usually write.
Can you tell me what my handwriting
says about me?
(Signature)

If you are obtaining a handwriting sample from someone else, be sure to use a new sheet of paper for each person. Incidentally, it's a good idea to collect some samples from other people to compare with yours. Since handwriting changes as a person gets older, try to get some samples from your friends or other kids your age. It can also be fun to look at your parents' handwriting, so you may want to ask them to give you samples too.

If you have your materials and a sample of your handwriting, you're ready to learn what your handwriting says about you. To do that, you need to look at the following clues hidden in the words you've written. Because it can be difficult to keep track of everything you find, it helps to record the information in the handwriting portrait chart on pages 145–46.

Be careful, however. If you haven't done your handwriting sample yet, you should stop reading here. Otherwise, your sample may be influenced by what you learn.

Baseline

The baseline is the line formed by the bottoms of most letters and of the pen strokes that connect them. If you were using lined paper, it's the line you'd want your letters to sit on. Of course, the idea here is to see where that line would be if you didn't have a printed line to follow. The slant and shape of your baseline are clues to *how you approach life.*

To find your baseline, place the tracing paper over your handwriting sample so that the two pages line up evenly. Then tape or staple the pages together at the top. This way, the tracing paper won't slip, but you can still lift it up if you need a clearer look at your sample. Remember to make all of your marks on the tracing paper, so that you don't mess up the sample.

Looking through the tracing paper, place your ruler underneath the bottom of the first letter and the bottom of the last letter in each line. In the case of the letters f, g, j, p, q, y, and z, ignore the part of the letter that loops down and use only the part that is ordinarily placed on the line. Then draw a straight line that joins these two points. (Although you can do this with a pen, it's better to use a pencil. That way, you can erase if you make a mistake.)

Find the baseline for each of the three lines in your sample. You can check the samples on pages 123–25 to make sure you're doing this correctly.

In which direction do the lines travel? Do they go straight across the page or do they slant up or down? Do the three lines go in the same general direction? Record the direction of your baseline in the column My Handwriting on your chart.

Next, draw a line under the bottom of each letter. Now connect the lines you've drawn. Do this for each of the three lines of the handwriting sample. If you have trouble figuring out how to do it, take a look at the samples on page 123.

What does your line look like? Is it pretty even, or does it jump up and down? If you're like many kids, it's probably somewhere in between. When you've decided what kind of shape your baseline has, enter that information on your chart too.

The slant and shape of your baseline provide different information about you. The slant of the baseline indicates *what you think about life in general and how you feel life is likely to treat you.*

Level

If your baseline travels straight across the page in a horizontal line, you have a realistic view of life. You don't expect rewards without working for them, but neither do you expect your efforts to fail. Although you know that you'll run into difficulties now and then, you feel that if you really try, you can work out most problems. Thus, you know you'll have to work for what you want, but you're pretty sure it will be worth the effort.

This is how I usually write. What does my handwriting say about me?

Upward Tilt

On the other hand, if your baseline slants up, you are an optimist. You feel that no matter what happens in your life, everything will work out for the best. This can be a very good trait, because it can make you willing to try new things without worrying about whether you'll fail. It also helps you deal with disappointments, since you tend to see them as only temporary setbacks.

This is the way I usually write. Can you tell me what my handwriting says about me?

However, being *too* much of an optimist can have some drawbacks. If you expect things to fall into your lap no matter what you do, you're not likely to put enough effort into your plans and dreams to make them happen. And if you think that everything is always going to work out for the best, you may avoid dealing with problems you should be paying attention to.

Downward Tilt

As you may have guessed, if your baseline slants downward, you are a pessimist. This means you have a gloomier view of life than either the realist or the optimist. You tend to feel that no matter what you do, somehow things are not likely to turn out well. If you're *very* pessimistic, you may think that everything you do is guaranteed to fail. Not surprisingly, pessimists often feel discouraged about ever really being happy or achieving the things they want. If

This is how I usually write. What does my handwriting say about me?

this describes you, you may want to talk to your parents, a teacher, or another adult you feel close to about your feelings. Expecting that you won't succeed, no matter what you do, makes it very difficult to try. Unfortunately, the less you try, the more likely it becomes that you *really* won't succeed.

On the other hand, if your baseline slants downward but you don't think you have a pessimistic view of life, you may be right. There can be other reasons for a downward baseline. Your handwriting reflects how you were feeling *at the time* you wrote your sample. If you were having a particularly rotten day or week, you may have been feeling unusually depressed or discouraged then. Feeling tired or ill can also give your baseline a downward slant.

Finally, if you wrote your sample on a small piece of paper, you may have felt you didn't have enough room. Sometimes, when people find they are reaching the edge of the page before they have finished a line, they slant their handwriting down to gain some extra space. This is one reason to make sure you get handwriting samples on a page that is 8½ by 11 inches.

Even or Uneven

The shape of your baseline—whether the letters form a straight or uneven line—is a clue to *how confident you feel about your goals and the steps you*

This is how I usually write .

What does my handwriting say about me?

This is how I usually write. What does hand writing say about me.

need to take to accomplish them. A generally firm baseline says that you know what you want and what you have to do to succeed. In contrast, an uneven baseline suggests that you are somewhat unsure about your goals or how to achieve them.

Of course, no one's baseline is perfectly straight, especially on unlined paper. And a few doubts now and then are not only natural, but healthy. But if your baseline jumps all over the place, you may be confused about where you are going and how to get there.

Add the meanings of your baseline slant and shape under the column What This Says About Me on your chart.

Angle or Slant of the Letters

The direction in which the letters of your handwriting lean indicates *how you deal with other people.* In measuring the slant of your handwriting, use only

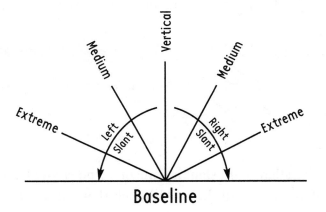

letters that have at least one straight side. The best are letters that extend above the others, such as d, h, l, and t, and those that drop below the line, such as y, g, and f (which does both), because they have the longest straight lines. However, you can also use the straight sides of some smaller letters, such as i, u, a, m, and n.

Place your ruler along the straight sides of these letters and draw the slant on your tracing paper. (You don't have to use every letter with a straight line, but choose enough to give you a good idea of the direction.) Next, compare the slant of these lines to your baseline. Do they lean to the right, to the left, or are they vertical compared to your baseline? If they do slant, it's important to know how much—slightly, moderately, or a lot? If you're not sure, check your slant against the guideline on the diagram above. Then add this information to your chart.

Right Slant

If your handwriting slants to the right, you like having other people in your life. The greater the slant, the more important others are to you.

A person with a slight right slant is someone who enjoys having friends and generally gets along well with them. Although these people like group activities, they probably spend more of their time with a few close friends.

A medium right slant is the sign of a party animal. If your handwriting slants moderately to the right, you have a greater desire for company. People with a medium right slant like being involved in a variety of social activities, such as going away to camp, joining clubs, or just hanging out with a bunch of friends. While people with a slight right slant occasionally enjoy doing things alone, those with a medium right slant aren't very happy going solo. They also have a greater need for attention, praise, and affection than someone whose handwriting slants only slightly to the right.

Of course, there is a difference between liking lots of people around and needing others desperately. An extreme right slant is a clue that the writer depends on other people too much. If your handwriting slants to the right *a lot,* then you tend to look to others to tell you what to do, what to want, and sometimes even who to be, instead of trying to figure out what *you* want and who *you* want to be.

Vertical

Vertical letters are written straight up, slanting in neither direction. Like their handwriting, people who write this way lean neither toward nor away from other people. If your handwriting is vertical, you have friends whom you like, but you're often just as content to be alone. Vertical writers are frequently described as being self-contained or self-sufficient—which is another way of saying that, in terms of social life, they find their own company quite good enough.

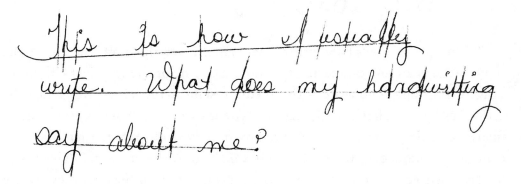

Left Slant

It's not very common to see handwriting with an extreme left slant, but many people's handwriting slants slightly or moderately to the left. If your handwriting slants to the left, you are more cautious about letting other people into your life—just how cautious depends on how much your letters slant. A slight left slant is the sign of someone who is often seen as being shy. People who write this way find it difficult to be outgoing and would much rather deal with others on a one-to-one basis than in a group. Because it's hard for them to open up and trust others, it takes these people a while to make friends. As you might expect, they don't usually enjoy school dances, giving a report in front of class, or going to the movies with five or six kids from their class.

this is how I usually write. what does my handwriting say about me?

The more a person's handwriting slants to the left, the more uncomfortable that person is around others and the more likely he or she is to feel left out or unwanted. People who write with a medium slant to the left are frequently described as loners. They usually have few friends whom they really trust, and in many cases they don't seem to have any friends at all. When a left slant becomes extreme, the writer is absolutely *sure* he or she isn't wanted. These people are positive that they will be hurt in dealing with others, so they isolate themselves completely.

When you've determined what the slant of your handwriting says about you, add this information to your chart.

Size

The size of your handwriting—how big the letters are—is an important clue to *your personality*. Like the baseline slant, handwriting size can be influenced by how much room the writer has, since most people write smaller when they need to fit a lot of words on a little piece of paper. Hopefully, you followed the advice at the beginning of the chapter and used a large enough sheet of paper so that you didn't feel cramped. On the other hand, if you're trying to analyze a sample written on a little scrap of paper, keep this in mind when deciding if the script is large, medium size, or small.

Learning to write is a skill that takes time to develop. Because it requires more physical control to write small, the handwriting of younger children is often larger than that of older kids. That's why it's a good idea to have samples of handwriting from some friends who are your age to compare your sample with.

If your handwriting sample is squished in a corner at the top of the page, it's obviously small. On the other hand, if it's all over the page, it's clearly large. The trick is making a decision about writing that falls in between these two extremes. The best way to do this is to compare your handwriting with other samples—perhaps from your parents as well as your friends—and use your judgment.

Large

Understanding the meaning of different sizes of handwriting is relatively easy. People who like to write large generally like to live large. They tend to be confident, friendly, fun-loving, outspoken, full of energy, and eager for new experiences. They also want a lot of attention and recognition. In short, if your handwriting is large, there's little chance that you're a shy, bashful kid.

Those who write large have a hard time doing tasks that they find monotonous and boring. They also aren't great at things requiring a lot of attention to detail. But their energy, enthusiasm, and willingness to try new things often help them to be successful in situations where creativity and imagination are called for.

This is how I usually write. What does my handwriting say about me?

Of course, there's large and then there's LARGE. If your handwriting is all over the place, you probably are too. You may be trying to do too much and have spread yourself too thin. Since the size of a person's script reflects the amount of attention he or she wants, you may also be overly concerned with being noticed by others.

Medium

The writer of a medium-size script is a balance of large-script and small-script traits. As a result, the medium-script writer is the most adaptable. If your handwriting fits this description, you're conscientious and careful and can handle tasks that are repetitious. But you can also be creative and versatile when you need to be. You are also likely to be truly interested in the feelings and concerns of the people around you. Although often described as "average," folks like you are the glue that holds the world together.

This is how I usually write.

What does my handwriting say about me?

Small

People whose handwriting is small tend to live in their own little worlds. They are happy focusing on their own particular interests and aren't terribly concerned with outside events or other people. If your handwriting is small, you like to analyze problems and can concentrate completely on finding the answers. In addition to your precision, desire for accuracy, and analytical abilities, you are often very creative. Thus, it's no surprise that many brilliant scientists and inventors have had small handwriting.

This is how I usually writ. What does my handwriting say about me?

Like extremely large writing, extremely small handwriting can be an indication that the writer is having some problems. In this case, the person is in danger of withdrawing completely from the world. A very small script may also signal a person who is trying to escape attention altogether—someone who hopes no one will notice them at all.

Pressure

Pressure is a measure of the force used in writing—that is, whether the writer pushed down hard on the pen, skimmed lightly across the page, or fell somewhere in between. Pressure is probably the easiest handwriting clue to determine, since the harder a person presses down when writing, the thicker and darker the letters will be. The amount of pressure or energy you put into writing is a sign of the amount of energy you are willing and able to put into the other things you do. Therefore, it's a very good clue to how much *determination* you have to achieve your goals.

One reason why handwriting samples should be written with a ballpoint pen is that the tip won't break if the writer presses down hard. People generally have the sense not to push down too hard when using a pencil, a felt-tip marker, or a fountain pen, so these writing tools may not give you an accurate sample.

In addition to seeing how thick and how dark the writing is, you can often measure pressure by running your hand across the back of the paper the sample is written on. If the writer used a lot of pressure, you can feel the letters with your fingers. You may also be able to see the imprint of the writing on the page underneath.

Besides determining how much pressure was used, look to see if the level of pressure was consistent. In other words, is the thickness or darkness of the letters the same across the page or is it lighter in some places and heavier in others?

This is how I usually write. What does my handwriting say about me?

This is how I usually write. What does my handwriting say about me?

This is how I usually write. What does my hand- writing say about me?

Firm/Heavy

If your handwriting pressure is firm or heavy, you have a lot of determination and put a good deal of effort into the things you do. Since people who try harder are more likely to succeed, those who use firm pressure in writing are more likely to achieve their goals. On the other hand, too much pressure is usually not a good sign. For example, people who use so much pressure that they actually tear the paper are often the same folks who think force is the answer to everything.

Moderate

Script written with a moderate amount of pressure is an indication of a person who is even-tempered and cooperative. If this is the way you write, you know how to balance your energy to achieve the things you want, but you don't try to force your decisions or plans on others.

Light

People who don't put much effort into their writing probably don't put much energy into the other things in their life either. If your handwriting pressure is light, you may be a quiet, gentle, or shy person whose style is just not very forceful. Not everyone wants fame and fortune, and you may be one of those who don't. On the other hand, you may have difficulty deciding on your goals and therefore see little reason to work hard to achieve them.

There is also the possibility that you didn't have much energy when you wrote your handwriting sample. If you were tired or not feeling well at the time, your handwriting pressure may have been lighter than usual. And if you are chronically ill, your handwriting pressure may always be light.

Writers whose pens barely touch the paper at all are telling the world that they hope both they and their faint handwriting will escape notice. Since they put very little effort, if any, into what they do, even the smallest obstacle can stop them dead in their tracks.

Even or Uneven

Putting a lot of energy into what you do is of little use if you can't keep it up long enough to finish a task. Pressure that starts out firm at the beginning of a handwriting sample but becomes noticeably lighter in places shows writers who aren't able to sustain the level of energy they started with. On the other hand, an even level of pressure is a sign of writers who are able to use the energy they have without burning out too soon.

If you haven't done so already, be sure to include the information about the size and pressure of your handwriting on your chart.

The Pronoun I

Words that relate specifically to you are called identity words. The most important of these is the pronoun I. When people use this word, it's very clear to them and to everyone else that they are talking about themselves. Thus, the way in which you write the pronoun I indicates *what you think of yourself.*

This is how I usually write. What does my handwriting say about me?

"I" taller than other capital letters

This is how I usually write. What does my hand writing say about me

"I" same height as other capital letters

This is how I usually write.

What does my handwriting say about me?

"I" shorter than other capital letters

In English, a word is capitalized to indicate it is important, either because it begins a sentence or because it is the name of a particular person or place. Look at the I in your handwriting sample. Is the height of this letter the same as the other capital letters, or is it taller or smaller? If your I is the same height as other capitals or is slightly taller, it means that you think you're at least as important as other important things in the world. A strong I is the sign of a person who has a good self-image and feels like a worthwhile human being. On the other hand, an I that is smaller than other capital letters is a clue that the writer doesn't feel he or she is important, or at least not as important as other people.

The slant of the I can be another clue to a person's self-image, if it differs from the slant of the rest of the handwriting. With what you've learned already, you can probably guess what it means when the I slants backward, while the rest of the handwriting slants to the right. A general right slant indicates that this person likes people and wants to move toward them. However, the left-slanting I shows that the writer is holding back, probably from a fear of being hurt. On the other hand, how would you interpret a right-slanting I in a script that generally slants to the left? One guess is that this person may be much friendlier than he or she seems.

The degree to which the I slants—even if it slants in the same direction as the rest of the script—also tells you something. For example, when the I leans farther to the right than the rest of the letters, it is a sign that the person is even more dependent on others than it appears on the surface.

By combining information about the size and slant of the I, you can get an even better picture of how the writer views him- or herself. How would you interpret an I that slants the same amount to the left (in this case, slightly) as the rest of the script, but is much smaller than the other capital letters? A slight left slant in general indicates that this person is cautious in making friends and relating to others, while the small I suggests that this hesitation may be due to a low self-image and a feeling of not being very worthwhile.

What does the pronoun I in your handwriting sample say about your own self-image and feelings of self-worth? If you don't think the answer fits you, you may want to look at other things you've written, such as letters, school essays, etc., in which you've used the word I. After all, your handwriting sample contains only one I, and perhaps it isn't typical of the way you usually form the word. But if the I's in other examples of your handwriting are similar to your sample I, perhaps you should give more thought to what your handwriting is trying to tell you.

Signature

Your signature also says something important about your image. Even kids who are just beginning to write intuitively know this—that's why they spend so much time experimenting with different ways to sign their name. In fact, if you're old enough to be reading this book, you've probably practiced your signature hundreds of times in order to get it to look exactly right.

In contrast to the pronoun I, which tells you how you see yourself, the way in which you write your name indicates *how you want others to see you*. Your signature is a way of presenting your name—and yourself—to the world. In the same way that many people wear particularly nice clothes when they want to make a favorable impression on others, they may also decide to "dress up" their signature.

Take a look at your signature and compare it to the rest of your handwriting sample. Is it similar to your general handwriting or does it differ in slant or size? How do the capital letters in your signature compare with the other capitals in your sample?

Similar

If your signature is similar to the rest of your handwriting, you're a "what you see is what you get" kind of person. You're comfortable having others know who you really are and don't feel a need to present yourself any differently.

Different Slant

In contrast, a signature that slants in a different direction from the rest of your handwriting suggests that you are trying to paint a picture of yourself that differs from your actual personality. People whose signatures slant to the right, while the rest of their handwriting slants to the left, are attempting to appear friendlier and more outgoing than they actually feel. On the other hand, if a person's signature slants to the left while the rest of the script slants to the right, he or she is friendlier than it seems but for some reason is holding back or covering up these feelings.

Different Size

It's probably obvious that people whose signatures are considerably bigger than the rest of their writing want their signatures—and themselves—to get attention. The larger the signature, the more attention the person wants. A really big signature is similar to a voice screaming, "Notice me!" Signatures that are smaller than the rest of the script are a sign of people who prefer not to attract attention. This may be because they just don't need much personal recognition, but it may also be because they don't feel very good about themselves.

Fancy Signatures

Signatures that are noticeably fancier than the rest of the script are an attempt to impress others. In addition to drawing attention, adding swirls or flourishes is a way of making the signature—and hopefully the writer—look less ordinary. This doesn't mean that you shouldn't care what your signature looks like. In fact, it's normal to want to present yourself in a positive light. But if your signature is much more elaborate than the rest of your handwriting, you may want to think about why you need to try so hard to impress other folks.

Finally, remember to include on your chart what you learned about the way you write the pronoun I and your signature.

A Signature Sampler

If this sample of signatures from the Declaration of Independence is any indication, the men who signed it must have had very different personalities. For example, from the size of his signature and the elaborate flourish under his name, you might guess that John Hancock craved attention and worked hard to be noticed—and you would be right. In fact, Hancock was a vain and flamboyant man who was fond of showing off his wealth. In contrast, John Adams's signature is simple, clear, and to the point—just what you'd expect from a man who was known to be blunt and outspoken.

What do you make of Thomas Jefferson's signature? Compared to the others, it is relatively large, with a slight to medium slant to the right. This indicates that he was confident, friendly, and full of energy, and that he liked people and wanted their attention and praise. Yet, his signature has none of the fancy swirls seen on many of the other signatures, suggesting that he wasn't concerned with impressing people. Although many of the other signatures are written with a firm, heavy pressure, Jefferson's signature seems to skim lightly across the page. Usually this indicates that the writer lacks determination or has a quiet, gentle personality. If these clues seem to provide conflicting information, there's a good reason why. Like his signature, Thomas Jefferson was a complex mixture of contradictions, a man who combined a remarkably bold mind with a highly sensitive nature.

Putting It All Together

If you look at the information you recorded in the column What This Says About Me, you can see what your handwriting says about the person you are today. Do you think this portrait resembles you? If you also analyzed the handwriting of some other people, do their descriptions seem to fit them? Did you learn anything about yourself that you think might be true but that you weren't aware of before?

If so, you may want to find out more about deciphering the many other clues in your handwriting. In the back, you'll find a list of some books that can help you use these clues to get an even better look at yourself.

My Handwriting Portrait

Clue	My Handwriting	What This Says About Me
Baseline		
Even or uneven:		
Horizontal, tilts up, or tilts down:		
Slant of the Letters		
Right (slight, medium, or extreme):		
Vertical:		
Left (slight, medium, or extreme):		
Size		
Large, medium, or small:		

Clue	My Handwriting	What This Says About Me
Pressure		
Firm, moderate, or light:		
Even or uneven:		
Pronoun I		
Size compared to other capital letters:		
Slant compared to the rest of the script:		
Signature		
Similar to the rest of the script:		
Slant is different:		
Size is different:		
Fancier than the rest:		

Index

A

C

colors *(continued)*
    mauve, 73
    orange, 74, 77
    purple, 73
    red, 73–74
    violet, 73
    yellow, 71–72
constellations, 2

D

Declaration of Independence, 142–44
Dog, 87–89, 107–8, 112–16
    on ascendant, 116
    relationships and, 97, 100, 103, 104, 108
    in triangle of affinity, 92
Dragon, 87–89, 99–100, 112–16
    on ascendant, 116
    relationships and, 95, 100, 105, 108
    in triangle of affinity, 90–91, 95

E

elementary hand, 43, 44, 46–47
elements, 3–4, 90
expression number, 78–84

F

G

M

R

S

harmonious vs. conflicting, 3–5
mutable, 5
oppositions of, 4–5, 7–8, 10, 11, 14, 15, 18, 19, 21–22, 23, 24, 26, 28, 30
water, 3, 4
see also specific Sun signs

T

Taurus: the Bull, 8–10, 27, 34, 35
    careers and, 9
    as earth sign, 4, 8, 9–10, 17, 24, 26
    as fixed sign, 5, 8, 10, 15, 21, 28
    relationships and, 9–10, 14, 15, 17, 21–22, 26, 28, 30
thumb, 41, 55–56, 57, 61
    of elementary hand, 44
Tiger, 87–89, 96–97, 100, 112–16
    on ascendant, 116
    relationships and, 96, 97, 99, 101, 103, 105, 108
    in triangle of affinity, 92

U

Uranus, 2